Selling with Silk Gloves, Not Brass Knuckles

A Guide to Winning Relationships

NORMAN G. LEVINE

Library of Congress Cataloging-in-Publication Data

Levine, Norman G.
   Selling with silk gloves, not brass knuckles : a guide to winning relationships / Norman G. Levine.
      p.   cm.
   ISBN 1-55874-466-5 (trade paper)
   1. Selling.   I. Title.
HF5438.25.L475   1997   96-30053
658.85—dc21   CIP

Cover design by Andrea Perrine Brower
Cover photo ©1996 PhotoDisc, Inc.

To the many friends, peers and confidants—some of whom are no longer with us—who gave me their special gifts of friendship, wisdom, inspiration, love and support. The cumulative effect of their mentoring and sharing converted a potentially hazardous and difficult journey through life's trials and tribulations into a joyous trip of achievements and relationships.

Among these many fellow travelers, one in particular has been an extraordinary partner and friend. To my wife Sandy, my very special thanks, appreciation, respect and love. Without her support my life, my career and this book would never have happened.

Mission Statement*

Why this book? Success and one's ability to sell oneself are interdependent.

Success demands that we concurrently sell ourselves both to ourselves and to others.

Though only those compensated directly for their selling activities are usually perceived as salespeople, everyone—regardless of their position in life, and often without realizing it—is selling to someone, every day.

Despite this truth, very few people—unfortunately, including many professional salespeople—excel at selling skills, which simply stated is their ability to influence others. Just a few examples of people influencing others include: parents, teachers, doctors, politicians, employers, etc.

*Mission statement—Successful individuals and companies have a vision of where they are, what they are doing, and where they are going. This vision should be written down to become their mission statement. It's a guide and should be revisited regularly. Though I have never seen a mission statement for a book, it seemed appropriate to have one to give the reader an understanding of "why this book" and secondarily, to illustrate and encourage the use of mission statements.

This book's mission is to share the secrets of successful selling (influencing): to help both the career salesperson reach new heights of success and all readers, regardless of their position in life, improve their effectiveness in favorably influencing their daily interpersonal relationships.

Using "silk gloves, not brass knuckles" should help you to have more fun, with less stress, while enjoying greater success. Hence this book. I hope you enjoy it.

Norman G. Levine

Contents

Chapter 2: Personal Attitudes

Chapter 3: Well-Being

Chapter 4: Goals and Dreams

Chapter 5: Planning

Chapter 6: Developing Relationships

Chapter 10: Making the Sale

Chapter 11: Client Services

Chapter 12: Systems and Procedures

Acknowledgment

Special thanks to my friend and associate, Owen Helms. Without his effort and commitment, this book would not have been successfully completed.

Blueprint for Success

- Personal attitudes influence effectiveness.
- Goals must be planned to be achieved.
- Career aspirations should be never-ending.
- Start at the beginning.
- Stay positively focused and optimistic.
- Always be prepared.

While my life has been dedicated to the techniques of selling, this book has been written for anyone whose livelihood depends on establishing relationships.

Whether you are selling a product, championing a cause or promoting yourself, the ultimate key to success with others is your own self-esteem.

Once you have finished reading the chapters, turn to the guide at the back. Any questions you may encounter in your quest for excellence should be easily cross-referenced to the table of contents. This will allow you to locate and diagnose the problem.

Action Projects have been included as work projects. The answers you give will change over time as your attitudes and confidence reach higher levels.

Any part of this book can be a source of reference, a refresher, a motivator or simply a resource. It can become the catalyst for increased personal effectiveness, now and for the indefinite future.

Schematic of a Successful Person

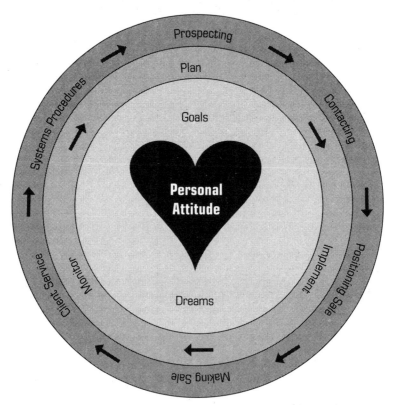

Read this schematic from the inside out.

- The heart of every successful person's effectiveness is his personal attitudes.
- These then influence the person's dreams. From these dreams the person establishes goals for each aspect of his life.

- This leads to a specific plan for achieving each goal. Next individual plans are implemented. Monitoring the individual results and performances leads to adjusted or new and more ambitious plans.
- The outer ring is primarily a schematic for salespeople. The person achieves the sales career goals by a never-ending process that begins with prospecting and eventually returns to more prospecting. This is repeated over and over again.

Preface

How do you approach life? With silk gloves or brass knuckles?

If you are in the business of selling a product, a cause or yourself, barging in and knocking down the prospective client won't get you far.

Building relationships is the key to success. During the last 50 years in business, I have found the smooth approach works far more effectively than the knock-down sucker punch.

Everybody is, in essence, a salesperson, even though a relatively small percentage get paid for selling.

People influence people. That's selling. Whether the dynamics involve a multi-million-dollar merger or the purchase of a new bed, interpersonal relationships are involved. This book will share concepts that will enhance a person's success. The contents are intended to be valuable to everybody.

Successful people, regardless of their profession, are winners only if they can effectively sell themselves to others. This vitality can lead to meaningful, mutually beneficial associations.

Happiness is the direct result of prosperous connections and one's own self-esteem. Happy people feel and act like winners.

Unfortunately, there are too few really happy people—hence too few winners.

Most people have it backwards. They seek happiness through financial success. It's the other way around. High self-esteem and a positive attitude will usually lead to prosperity.

Also, we must eliminate the word "try." The word itself suggests the possibility of failure. It's the first step toward a self-fulfilling prophecy of mediocrity.

If you want something, don't TRY. Go GET it.

Winners do, others try. If you don't already agree, please keep an open mind as you read along. Let us begin by letting me illustrate how the key to success is selling relationships.

Think about these examples:

- A husband tries to convince his wife to make a decision or vice versa.
- Parents try to get children to conform to their basic values and rules.
- Children try to get permission for something they would not normally be allowed to do.
- A physician recommends a certain procedure for the patient's well-being.
- An attorney settles a claim.
- An employer gets an employee to conform to procedure.
- An employee influences the employer's decision.
- A job applicant completes a successful interview.
- A politician runs for public office.
- People debate publicly or privately over important issues.
- Boy meets girl; girl meets boy.

What do these scenarios have in common?
THEY'RE ALL SELLING!

Every interpersonal relationship involves influencing or motivating someone. To achieve true empathetic relationships, certain skills should be utilized.

Although the ideas in this book were developed from my sales experiences, those same ideas—when converted to skills in action—can help in everyday life.

Anyone can become more effective by fine-tuning his interpersonal skills. This will almost always involve some degree of selling.

Professional salespeople, whose compensation is dependent on making sales, will find the skills discussed in this book invaluable for positively impacting on their careers. However, as for all successful people, it begins with selling *yourself*.

Most people are not successful or effective in their relationships because (a) they don't know how, (b) they won't pay the price.

To illustrate with a story: A religious congregation in a poor area was seeking a new minister. They found the perfect candidate, but they were concerned that the minister might not accept the position because of the low pay. To their surprise, he said he would enjoy the opportunity to serve. The church spokesman said they couldn't afford a big house, however, they would find a handyman's special and all the congregants would help fix it up.

The minister accepted. When he arrived, the congregation found a house that was truly in shambles. Keeping their promise, the church members pitched in and transformed an eyesore into a lovely home.

The minister was in the garden working on his roses when a stranger came by and admired his home and garden.

He said, "Minister, this place is truly beautiful. Isn't it amazing what the good Lord can bring forth?"

The minister smiled and said, "You're absolutely right, my son, but you should have seen this house and garden when the good Lord was taking care of it all by himself."

This isn't intended as a religious story but it does illustrate a point. We are all born with God-given gifts that present us with the opportunity to take our "fixer upper" lives and make them anything we want them to be.

Sitting back and waiting for others to make things happen will not give us fulfillment and happiness. On the other hand, by using our natural gifts and talents, we can realize all our dreams and expectations. Just as the house was transformed, we, too, will develop into beautiful human beings who bring joy to those around us and happiness and fulfillment to ourselves.

For many who are frustrated because they fail to utilize their natural talents, the logical excuse is to blame the environment rather than themselves.

To illustrate with a story: A farmer in the Midwest dreamed of having the best seed corn in the world. From his efforts, he hoped to achieve pride and self-esteem. Each spring and summer he worked hard and long. Each fall he took his best seed corn to the county fair.

His hard work and discipline paid off. Every year he won the blue ribbon. Then after the fair each year, he shared his prize-winning seed corn with his immediate neighbors, who were also his competitors at the county fair.

One year a neighbor asked, "Since you're so competitive, I don't understand why you share your best corn with us. Don't you know you put us in a better position to beat you?"

The champion seed-corn farmer responded with a chuckle. "You don't know very much about farming, do you?" he said.

He explained that to have the best seed corn, he couldn't have poor strains of corn growing in the fields next to his. This would lower the grade of his corn the following year. He added that he was happy to share his best so each of his neighbors could also have quality corn and prosper. He knew the corn he grew would be interbreeding with top-quality seed. He also knew that if he worked a little harder, he could once again win the blue ribbon.

It is a cop-out to blame others for our troubles. Even in adverse situations, positive thinking, sharing with others and living by the Golden Rule will help contribute to our own success and joy—and the happiness of others.

This philosophy is applicable to everyone but especially to salespeople. During times of frustration and disappointment—compounded by intense competition—it is tempting to bend the rules, to overstate, to make promises that will be unfulfilled and misrepresent products and/or services.

At those times it is easy to denigrate the competition. Such action damages the person expressing those feelings as much or more than the object of their attack. However, a common commitment to integrity, trust, honesty, support, sharing and caring improves effectiveness. Everyone benefits.

Happiness is different things to different people. But here is a general formula:

self-esteem + relationships = happiness

Self-esteem is heavily influenced by personal pride, self-confidence, respect, success and achievement.

Relationships should be positive and mutual. They include family, friends, business associates, school and community.

Each of us reacts with joy or sadness, depending upon our own self-measurement and self-judgement in these two areas.

Effective selling—whether used for business or for personal purposes—depends upon our self-confidence and positive mental self-perceptions. Achieving happiness and our ability to sell are both dependent on self-esteem and relationships.

Though many schools, books and seminars feature interpersonal skills, they often miss the key point. Anyone can learn to sell. Techniques can be taught. But too often the student lacks the necessary attitudes, skills, motivation or understanding to implement them.

Like happiness, selling is different things to different people. It is even different things to the same people at different times.

While every salesperson doesn't have to be world class, the more skillful the person, the more persuasive he or she will be. Though natural talent is an important part of selling and fulfillment, almost anyone who is willing to learn and then practice the skills will succeed.

In my long professional career, which included selling, training and influencing other people, it always frustrated me to see so many gifted people struggle when they could have been thriving. This book should help each reader reach higher levels of accomplishment in their chosen persuasion by highlighting issues that may have inhibited their self-fulfillment.

Occasionally I try to motivate the unmotivated, though I know that it is often a fool's errand. Most people must want something badly enough to pay the price of getting it. However, I have seen people change. It is my hope that most readers will already be self-motivated and are seeking a road to follow. If not, perhaps this book will help them find a reason to take the first step towards a greater tomorrow. Nobody said change was easy. However, if the rewards are great enough, and the methods required to get those rewards are clearly understood, growth is realistically attainable.

This book will help identify and solve blind spots or problems, but unfortunately, there is rarely one simple solution to any given problem.

Therefore, readers should select the concepts and methods that fit their unique situation and mentally file away, for future reference, those that are not appropriate for the instant need.

While each of us is unique, one basic belief holds true for all: Positive mental attitudes and realizing your dreams are the foundations for success in anything you choose to do.

1

Attributes of Successful People

A.1: AN OVERVIEW

Before getting to this book's in-depth consideration of the attributes of most successful people, let me share an overview of some of those traits that are often overlooked and rarely taught. Hence, I refer to them as a "hidden curriculum." From these traits comes self-discipline and, thus, people who are empowered. To help us remember these strengths. The majestic eagle can give us two acronyms using the bird's most powerful body parts, the beak and talons.

B = Belief
E = Enthusiasm
A = Activity
K = Knowledge

T = Talent

A = Attitude

L = Love

O = Organized *(see chapter 12)*

N = Natural attributes (the 8 M&M's)
- Mental alertness
- Medical and physical well-being *(see chapter 3)*
- Maturity
- Morality
- Monetary discipline
- Marital stability
- Motivation *(see chapter 4)*
- Mentoring

S = Skillfulness *(see entire book)*

Except where otherwise noted, I will briefly elaborate on these attributes in the balance of this chapter.

A.2: BELIEF

In order to feel good about what we do, no matter what our profession, we must believe in ourselves. We have to believe in the community in which we live, in our families and in our ability to be anything we want to be. It is essential to commit to a cause and be proud of it. If we don't, how can we believe in ourselves?

People who aspire to lofty goals, but who have trouble reaching them, must have two important traits: (1) a belief that they can win, and (2) the willingness to change, if necessary.

Successful people believe in what they do. They believe in the ideas and products they promote. They believe they provide a unique service for their clients. This idealistic belief may be hard for some people to understand. It's not something that's purely business-motivated. It's a sincere belief which makes them feel good about what they do.

A.3: ENTHUSIASM

Frank Bettger, author of *How I Raised Myself from Failure to Success,* said: "You've got to act enthusiastic to be enthusiastic. You've got to act successful to be successful."

It took me a while to fully appreciate the depth and meaning of that statement. But there is absolutely no question that successful people acted successfully before they became successful. They act enthusiastic, even when they don't feel great. I've never seen a dynamic loser and I've never seen a superstar who doesn't have a sparkle in his or her eye. The dynamism, the power, the excitement of spirited, successful people stirs action. The same cannot be said of laid-back, passive, contemplative, reactive people. If we don't act like we want to be, we will never get where we want to be.

If exhibiting fervor means screaming at the top of your lungs in your car before going into a meeting, or shrieking "I can do it! I can do it!" before a sales pitch, then *do it.* Do whatever it takes to get the adrenaline flowing.

All too often, it's not *what* is said, it's *how* it's said. People are most influenced by people they perceive as winners. Winners act like winners. You must be positive, eager, dynamic, every moment of your life, even when you don't feel that way. You must carry yourself like the successful person you hope to be. Not only will the public's perception be far more positive but your own effectiveness will be multiplied because of your self-confidence, enthusiasm and self-esteem.

The great majority of people (salespeople included) are passive to negative. That is how they come across. They remember the sales lost, not sales made. They are sensitive to the objections to their product or cause and not excited about the positives. They are concerned with the cost of the product, not the value it represents.

Writers are easily discouraged by rejection. But the best and brightest received hundreds of rejections before being published—that includes greats like Jack London and Mark Twain.

Defeat is a self-fulfilling prophecy.

Remember the movie *Field of Dreams*? The theme revolved around building a baseball field in the middle of a large cornfield. The premise was: "If you build it, they will come." It may have been pure entertainment but it holds true for many professions, especially sales.

"Believe you will sell it and they will buy."

A.4: ACTIVITY—A GAME OF NUMBERS

The number one reason for failure is not enough effort. How many voters must a politician reach to be elected? How many publishers must a writer submit a manuscript to before acceptance? How many interviews must the salesperson have to achieve a goal? With all of these examples, the end result is based on averages.

The work ethic, the self-discipline, the energy and the zeal necessary to achieve these objectives are all attributes of world-class achievers. If you don't have them already, they must be learned and put into action.

Therefore, no one would ever fail if they simply realized success is a direct function of effort and the level of necessary activity. For example, though one salesman might successfully sell one prospect in three, while another one person in 10, they would end up with the same number of sales if the one in 10 salesperson had the same number of tens as the other had of threes.

Regardless of your persuasion, winners classically put in more effort and have more activity than their average peer.

A.5: KNOWLEDGE

Many people who achieve modest success are not necessarily experts in their fields. They are gifted people who work hard to promote their ideas, their egos or their products. That can be enough to make a person successful and/or a super salesperson. Although activity, combined with hard work and basic skills, might help a person survive and excel, the truly gifted persuaders are also experts in their field.

I learned this lesson the hard way.

I had become moderately successful as a commissioned insurance salesman. Even though I wasn't in the so-called "Big Leagues," I was reasonably well-known. I thought I was satisfied.

In the early 1970s I was the opening speaker at a sales meeting in Indiana. The theme of my talk was, You Can Be Anything You Want to Be. The crowd reaction was positive.

The next speaker was notable and eventually became the president of the company he represented. Wherever he traveled he encouraged all people to raise their professionalism by getting appropriate academic degrees. He was a very good friend of mine and knew I didn't have any business-related diplomas and felt that was the reason I wasn't as successful as I could have been.

In front of an audience of 1,000 people, he said: "Norman, if you can be anything you want to be, how come you don't have any academic designations after your name?"

I blurted out, "You're right, Bob, I guess I should."

Without missing a beat, he said, "I know you should, but will you?"

Without carefully considering a response and with 1,000 people listening, I blurted out, "Yes."

I know I'm more motivated by the fear of failure than I am by the achievements of success. With my promise to Bob, in front of a large audience, I had no choice but to get an appropriate designation. I can't remember working so hard at something I didn't want to do. I consolidated a five-year educational program into one year. Bob gave me the greatest gift a person can give another person: the will to strive for more. I achieved my first academic designation in one year.

With increased self-confidence, as well as the expertise that came from new-found knowledge, my average size sale increased dramatically. So did my income! All without my working any harder.

The kind of instruction people need is heavily dependent on what they do. The foundation for becoming an "expert" is education. However, knowledge by itself isn't enough. Nobody serves their field of endeavor by becoming well-educated failures. You must maintain a level of adequate skills, work disciplines, activity and then if you add knowledge and expertise, you will dramatically improve your productivity and career growth. You could say knowledge is the engine, but the gas is skill and activity.

A.6: TALENT

Natural talents are rarely mentioned as a prerequisite for success. There are two reasons:

First, God-given gifts are beyond our control.

Second, the great majority of people—perhaps everybody reading this book—have the capacity to do better!

Simply stated, each of us will reach a proficiency level determined by our desire, attitude, commitment, enthusiasm and work ethic.

Some talents enhance our capacity to perform; others detract. The probability of success is enhanced by the capacity to communicate effectively, whether by voice or by action. Look at some of the most highly esteemed actors. They can make you laugh or cry, they evoke every emotion possible.

Every profession has a certain degree of negativity and rejection. The ability to be resilient—to take the criticism and come back for more—is a great asset. Think about the bashing politicians take; take a look at movie and book reviews. That rejection may be hard to take. But it doesn't stop the world from going around.

Desire and work ethic can compensate for most shortcomings. You can be anything you want to be, if you are prepared to take the bad with the good and a risk now and then.

By being objective about your natural talents, you have every reason to believe you will achieve moderate levels of success. There are very few impossible missions because the differences between success and failure are almost always things over which we have some control.

A.7: ATTITUDE

Everyone agrees Positive Mental Attitude (PMA) is a require-ment for victory. Active PMA, coupled with visible enthusi-asm, is the fuel that powers most success stories. Here are some clues for overcoming negativity:

1. Most negative people will say, "I am not negative." But the absence of negativity does not make a positive per-son. A positive attitude is not passive. It requires action. Communicate positive and enthusiastic thoughts as much as possible.

2. The desire to be successful and to appear positive will not make one feel and appear positive unless you really have a PMA and actively demonstrate its presence.

3. Positive people have empathy and compassion for oth-ers. They act with strength, conviction and direction. They have the courage to say no when necessary.

4. Bad-mouthing competition or denigrating others will not enhance one's image. Respecting and commenting on the good traits of others adds to one's stature. If you can't say something good, don't say anything.

5. Complaining, seeking pity or putting oneself down (self-deprecating behavior) does not promote respect. Positive talk does.

6. People who can easily be dominated will not grow into strong successes; they will communicate weakness. Ambitious individuals who respect other people for their talents, rather than their position, will develop into suc-cessful people.

7. Compromising one's standards by accepting relation-ships with unethical and immoral associates destroys

one's professional position. Spend time with other winners whenever possible.

8. People motivated by selfishness will, generally speaking,
   not be successful and accepted.

A.8: LOVE

When Jim Longley, the independent governor of Maine, died, he left many legacies. One of those was love. He had always lived a courageous life; he fought the toughest battle of his life, terminal cancer, with unbelievable dignity.

Many of his friends kept in touch with him regularly during those final months. Because of the distance that separated us, we connected by telephone. After a while, he began to end every phone call with, "Thanks for calling, Norm. By the way, I love you." He said those words at the end of every conversation until he died.

At one point during a TV interview, Jim was asked, "What have you changed, now that you know you are going to die?"

"Not too much," he said. "But I spend more time with family and appreciate each moment more." He added that all his life he had been too macho to express sentimental emotions.

"Now, however, when I talk to someone I love, I tell them I love them because I know I may never have another chance." When I heard his answer all those phone calls flashed through my mind and helped change my life forever.

I learned that caring, compassion, empathy and love are part of becoming a world-class person. We all need love: in business, in selling, in family and in relationships with friends and associates. It is okay to say so.

Everyone in our lives, in and out of business, deserves to be appreciated for themselves. There are many levels and kinds of love, but empathetic relationships make both parties feel good. Feeling good about each other and ourselves is great for the soul. Happily, it is also good for business.

A.9: MENTAL ALERTNESS

Mental alertness can significantly impact overall effective-ness. However, even people who are mentally challenged can learn simple tasks and do them efficiently. I have always found such people delightful and dependable associates. However, their limitations usually come into play when they must think through a new situation for which they have not been adequately prepared.

This has taught me a great deal about success as it relates to mental capacity. To be an outstanding success, to have the ability to make quick decisions and to adapt to life's difficult situations, requires that you be teachable, adaptable and quick to react to the unexpected.

It's not necessary to be a genius, or even someone with an extremely high IQ. You must have the desire and ability to learn, the capacity to change quickly in a given situation, the expertise to adapt to specific circumstance and not insist on remaining on a rigid, preselected path, performing most key tasks by rote.

A.10: MATURITY

Maturity is not necessarily determined by chronological age. There are 60-year-old children and 21-year-old adults.

It's difficult to describe what makes a person appear to be competent and mature, but there is an instinctive reaction within all people that creates that opinionated judgment. In part it's the way people act, dress and live. It's their discretion, expertise and effectiveness in communicating and sharing wise counsel.

If maturity is not a natural part of your personality, it will require considerable effort to change. It is worth the effort. The positive impact is tangible. Trust and respect, which are essential for great success, cannot be earned by individuals who act both immature and/or irresponsible.

A.11: MORALITY

Opinion polls suggest that the consumer's perception of certain professionals indicates a low level of public esteem. Their ethics and business principles are questioned.

In every profession there are the good, the bad and the ugly. Some make newspaper headlines. Some are the butt of jokes and political cartoons. Every day the paper is filled with scams: stock market, pay phones, credit cards, travel agency ripoffs.

Individuals might be able to get away with cheating or misrepresenting for a short period of time, but if that is part of their regular existence, eventually they'll get caught or, at the very least, lose their public's confidence. Respect comes with trust and morality; we must each earn that admiration.

If you plan on a selling career or any persuasion that depends on interpersonal relationships, you must be absolutely straight, even in marginal areas, if you expect to build a respected reputation.

Occasionally you will meet people who will want to take shots at you and your reputation. You may be unable to avoid becoming a target, but only if you have twisted the principles of ethics and morality, will the attacker be able to knock you down. Sadly, in the short term, being honest will, on occasion, cost the salesperson sales. The good news is that, in the long run, you will succeed because the unethical competition will eventually get caught and fail.

Morality and public perception can also be an opportunity to make sweet lemonade from sour lemons. The public's negative perceptions can be used to enhance your career. Prospects who are suspicious of people in your industry are perfect prospects since their doubts make them particularly anxious to find someone they can trust. Capitalize on that by offering and delivering your professionalism, and by using friends and clients to spread the word of your honesty.

World-class people build their careers by doing the right thing right. They never respond in kind to avoid losing to someone unscrupulous. They know that value added to relationships is the substance of a solid career and that, despite occasional set-backs, eventually winners always win and losers always lose.

A.12: MONEY DISCIPLINES

Budgeting is an important part of life, whether you are an actor getting $12 million for a movie, or a clerk-typist earning minimum wage. Everyone should think of himself as the chief executive officer of his own being and bank account. We must learn to budget for all expenses necessary for sustaining both business and non-business requirements, as well as having a slush fund for emergencies.

Besides obvious current expenses, budgets should provide for taxes, unexpected expenses, insurance. A significant amount should be invested as part of a wealth-accumulation plan. Even if you are at a job where there is a retirement fund, anything can happen. In this day and age, layoffs are common and downsizing is rampant. Companies are slashing benefit plans right and left.

Being in control of your time and income potential is essential, especially for salespeople and anyone else who does not receive a steady paycheck.

All too often, salespeople and entrepreneurs can be irresponsible about money matters.

It is not uncommon for salespeople to spend more than they earn. In doing so they accumulate substantial debt while developing a pretentious standard of living. They assume that their income will continue to grow even though commission income is irregular at best.

Most salespeople want to enjoy the benefits of success too quickly. Competition with their peers contributes to this. The risk is great and a tremendous number of salespeople get into financial difficulty early in their career.

Even if they exhibit financial prudence and don't get into trouble, they rarely accumulate the necessary wealth for financial independence at retirement. It's surprising how many people don't accumulate money for emergencies, taxes, old age, even though they may be earning a substantial income.

Since salespeople are entrepreneurs and most entrepreneurs are salespeople, they cannot depend on the company pension plan as an adequate resource when their working days are over. They must provide for their own pension and health-related requirements. Even if there are company-provided plans, they are rarely sufficient to sustain the living standards to which one has become accustomed.

Since aspiring successful people may have higher-than-average income early in their career, the temptation to buy foolishly, push credit limits and live in luxury can lead to financial ruin. If you make a financial plan, work that plan. If you're not financially prudent, no matter how successful you are at a particular period in your career, you can ultimately face disaster.

You should have a wealth accumulation plan that will assure financial independence in the shortest possible time, based on your own unique situation.

A.13: MARITAL STABILITY

Any major emotional distraction or stress that takes away from our ability to concentrate on our career will negatively impact our effectiveness and success.

Some of these outside stresses are totally beyond our control: physical well-being, the economy, war, chaos, legislative changes. One situation that we can control is one that is often underrated: interpersonal and/or marital stability.

Whether single or married, the key word is stability.

Falling in or out of love, getting married or divorced, and fighting with a very special person in your life are all among the highest distractions to work effectiveness. They may be *the* highest, except for death and severe illness. We are not just sidetracked, we can be completely derailed. The instability of interpersonal relationships is potentially destructive to our career and, perhaps, our well-being.

Building a successful life or career requires total and complete attention and commitment. The stability issue should not be underrated. If you are in a highly volatile situation—a pending marriage or divorce, custody battle, whatever—wait until your affairs are in order before making any critical career decisions.

A.14: MENTORING

In 50 years of selling, I've been privileged to meet super greats in many different persuasions, as well as failures and everything in between. Interestingly, I have found that the great majority of really successful people have had a relationship with a mentor who significantly contributed to their success and well-being.

Some relationships were long distance, others involved daily contact. But they all had certain things in common: shared wisdom, inspiration and pep talks.

Mentoring can be done in many different ways, but most successful people have had a mentor who they, at least partially, credit with their own personal success and achievement.

The mentor also gains tremendous satisfaction, pride and significant self-motivation from watching a protégé attain new levels of achievement.

Most successful people respond favorably to ambitious, hardworking, aspiring career people who ask for help. A good friend of mine had a great expression: "To be a great success you learn by doing, you don't do by learning."

Classrooms and study aren't the best way to learn relationship selling. Watching an expert do it, and then doing it in front of the expert, is the best school available. For example, look at acting schools. They are often run by actors. Writing classes are given by writers; dancing lessons by retired dancers.

Let me strongly recommend that any truly hard-driving, ambitious person who is not achieving the results he wants to attain should seek help from an existing, matured person from his own world and try to work out some kind of ongoing relationship.

The best relationship would include working together. Even though this probably means splitting income, 50 percent of something is a lot better than 100 percent of nothing. The free education that comes with the experience is invaluable.

From the mentor's point of view, nothing is more exciting than working with someone aspiring and ambitious. I have seen seasoned salespeople go on a call with a younger associate and exhibit a level of excitement and enthusiasm they had not had in many years. There's nothing like an audience or a protégé to rekindle the sparks.

This relationship can be as formal or informal as the mentor and aspirant desire. It can be a breakfast session every other week, regular training sessions or anything in between. The key is reaching out and offering a hand.

This is a win-win deal. Mentors are inspired and motivated by the relationship with a protégé. There is great pleasure in the developing success of a younger person. At the same time, I have never met a novice who hasn't been inspired and gratified by the sharing and caring they received from a mentor.

There are some personality tests to determine complementary personalities. However, in real life it is often instinctive; two people know when they are "simpatico." Even if a mentoring relationship eventually fails, both sides have usually benefited from the relationship.

ACTION PROJECT

Power

Power is the key to effectiveness. Without it, mediocrity is the result.

Successful people capitalize on their own individual strengths. Each of us has identifiable traits that can be utilized in one way or another. It is our challenge to accentuate our strengths and minimize our weaknesses.

There is no single physical or personality type that assures power. It doesn't matter if we are short and soft-spoken or tall and dominating. Both can succeed and both can fail.

The following self-analysis questions can help you identify your strengths and weaknesses and determine if change is needed.

Evaluating your own strengths and weaknesses for each of the categories in the BEAK and TALONS acronyms should help you determine where you should concentrate some of your self-improvement efforts.

	Strength	Weakness	Change
B = **Belief.** Do you believe in yourself, career, product?	_____	_____	_____
E = **Enthusiasm.** Do you have enthusiasm for life, career, future?	_____	_____	_____
A = **Activity.** Is your activity enough to achieve personal goals?	_____	_____	_____

	Strength	**Weakness**	**Change**
K = Knowledge. Do you have adequate knowledge of business, clients, community?	_____	_____	_____
T = Talent. Are you using your talent effectively?	_____	_____	_____
A = Attitude. Is your attitude positive, optimistic?	_____	_____	_____
L = Love. Are you committed to family, career, employer?	_____	_____	_____
O = Organized. Are you efficient, organized?	_____	_____	_____
N = Natural attributes. Do you use your natural attributes?	_____	_____	_____
S = Skill. Do you have the necessary skills to perform well?	_____	_____	_____

2

Personal Attitudes

B.1: AN OVERVIEW

To be successful, basic knowledge, practices and procedures must be learned. That goes for any profession. A successful doctor must stay current with new trends and medicines. Attorneys must be aware of new legislation and landmark cases.

When someone has the desire and discipline to effectively implement the basics, it is likely that career survival and achievement will follow.

The most important single common denominator of all successful people is their extraordinary attitude.

Without a positive, active, enthusiastic, self-confident, goal-oriented mental attitude, achieving one's ultimate maximum potential is highly unlikely.

B.2: ATTITUDE

Survival and victory is a reflection of attitude. Success or failure lies in the capacity to control emotions, to work with intense self-discipline and to live each day with a strong, focused viewpoint and manner.

Since my expertise is in the world of selling, here are some thoughts on attitudes in sales. They are, however, universal messages that can be applied to life itself.

- You won't be effective with people with whom you are uncomfortable.
  —Stay in your world but upgrade it.
- You can't sell what you don't understand.
  —Expand your knowledge and skill.
- You won't become successful until you act that way.
  —Stop complaining and start boasting.
- You won't work hard unless you want the rewards.
  —Decide what you really want, then go for it.
- You won't be effective with winners if you are a loser.
  —Stop putting yourself and your business down.
- You won't look professional without practice.
  —Why make things look difficult when they're not?
- You won't get to know a lot of people without taking some risks.
  —Prospecting is more guts than talent. Get tough.
- You won't score big by goofing off.
  —Goof-offs pursue happiness but end up sad.
- You won't build a career on lies and dreams.
  —Admit your weaknesses and flaunt your strengths.

And remember:

- Accentuate the positive, eliminate the negatives.
- You won't be a star emulating losers.
- Travel with the best. Pick their brains.
- Solve your problems by helping others solve theirs.
- Empathy and compassion are the secrets of success.
- Activity + results = success.

B.3: HAVING FUN

No one goes from novice to superstar on a perfectly paved road. Bumps are there for everyone. It's those very humps that separate the superstars from ordinary folks. The good news is there is a way over, under or around them, if you really want to succeed and prosper.

Many bad moments may seem catastrophic, yet you don't remember them a month or a year later. These times are usually blown way out of proportion.

If you take yourself too seriously, or spend too much time worrying about the negatives, you suck the fun out of whatever you're doing. However, if you relish your victories, accept the defeats and consider it all a learning experience, you can have a good time.

- Dream big dreams and believe they will come true.
- Pace yourself and make time for family and recreation.
- Count your blessings and have fun.
- Work when you work, play when you play.

To say you should have fun as an aspiring successful person might almost appear sadistic, especially when you're in a sales slump or emotionally drained. Take heart from the fact that most successful people really love what they do. And remember, no matter what you do, everyone has slumps, depression and periods of wondering if they're in the right business.

We all have dues to pay before reaping the rewards. Ever notice how many grade B and C movies famous actors made before hitting the jackpot? How much time does a physician have to put in at miserly wages before he or she earns a decent income? How many books must an author write before getting a contract?

Think of going into business like joining a sorority or fraternity. There may be a hazing period, but, if you stick with it, the rewards are tangible. Not giving up is the key.

The negative person is less effective in whatever he does. The optimistic, dynamic, excited, upscale person is more effective. If we can't learn to have fun, we may never enjoy the maximum benefits of our chosen profession. Relax, smile, accept the lumps and bumps as part of life. See the glass as half full.

B.4: AT WHAT PRICE?

Although luck plays an important part, it's not the key to success. There are no free lunches. Of course it's possible to
win the lottery and become an instant millionaire, but the odds
are slim.

Prosperity is a relative thing. Some people are quite comfortable with moderate success and an unassuming standard of living. For others there are higher mountains to climb. Both can be
perceived as successful.

Consider a potential car buyer. If an individual wanted the
biggest and best car available, he'd visit a Rolls-Royce showroom.
But for most of us, a Rolls-Royce is attainable only if we are ready
to give up our home, clothes, food and entertainment.

On the other hand, there are some who are willing to sacri-
fice for the luxury of owning a Rolls. It's a matter of priority that
determines what price we're prepared to pay. That goes for
everything in life: home (rental or mansion), clothing (bargain
basement or hand-tailored), food (gourmet takeout or home-
cooked). You get the picture.

How high is the mountain you want to climb? Or are you content to take what comes?

The cost of mediocrity is significantly less than the cost of success. Of course prosperity cannot always be measured in dollars
and cents. Time, discipline and attitude are only a few of the
components. If there are no free lunches, then it also holds true
that the fancier the lunch, the higher the tab.

Perhaps this concept appears self-evident, but there's a flip side
that many people overlook. There is an additional, less obvious,
cost for mediocrity that is rarely considered, but it should be.

Most people want instant gratification: the grand house, the
luxury car, dining at fancy restaurants, trendy clothes. That's
why some people run a little faster, work harder. Unfortunately,

if they don't run hard enough, they will still be running 20, 30, 40 years later. Some people grow every year. Others start over again every year or two.

Why is that? Lack of self-esteem; a basic, draining unhappiness; lack of desire and enthusiasm all contribute to a general unhappiness and dissatisfaction.

Eventually these underachievers will look back and say, "If I had only . . ." But it will be too late. Sadly, mediocrity almost always assures a lack of dignity in old age. If a person barely makes ends meet while working (when his income is at its highest), his lifestyle will drop to submarginal levels when that income stops.

Immediate gratification is not the key. For a long, happy and prosperous life with dignity and self-respect, it is necessary to pay a price up front, then enjoy the rewards later. In the long run, the smaller price is the price of success. Ultimately mediocrity demands the highest price of all.

B.5: ADVERSITY—THE KEY TO CREATIVITY

The real test of greatness is how people react to adversity. It's easy to be a hero when everything's going well. But what happens when the heat is on full blast?

Nobody can live a full life without experiencing adversity. There are thousands of stories of courage and ingenuity. Here is one example of overcoming disaster.

Many years ago a salesman I was training decided to go skiing. Although he'd only been in the business two years, his life was going very well. Too bad he couldn't take his luck to the slopes. He came home in an ambulance. A large cast covered most of his lower body. He couldn't walk. It appeared to be a significant disruption to his career.

Under these trying circumstances, he refused to quit. On his own initiative he hired a full-time limousine and chauffeur. He made appointments. Then off he would go with his wheelchair, the limo and the driver.

He always apologized for the inconvenience and thanked the client for agreeing to see him. He was selling disability and life insurance; he was his own living testimonial! By turning adversity to advantage, his sales skyrocketed. By the time he was fully recovered he was an insurance superstar.

Most people in that same situation would have felt sorry for themselves and allowed failure to take over. The way you handle a challenge separates ordinary people from the extraordinary. Problems shouldn't be excuses for failure, but instead should be the foundation of success.

B.6: WHAT MAKES PEOPLE RUN?

Managers often select people who could be defined as pussycats because they are people who are easy to work with, easy to train, easy to discipline and easy to control. Unfortunately, pussycats generally do not make it to the big leagues. It's hard to be a pussycat in the office and a tiger in the field.

Tigers may bring in more business but they are difficult to control, difficult to train and difficult to discipline. There is no question that there are sweet, lovable, successful tigers. They are the exception. I'd rather find a tiger, pay the emotional price of training a difficult-to-handle employee and watch that big cat tear the opposition apart.

Self-confidence, independence, commitment, enthusiasm are part of a tiger's makeup. But what makes a tiger run?

Money is a great motivator. However, surprisingly few people really get turned on solely because of a check. Most tigers, despite their tough exterior, are sensitive people who are frequently more motivated by ego, lifestyle or recognition.

To be self-motivated, you must want a lifestyle, an image or material rewards. It is also absolutely essential to know what your goals and objectives are. That is the ultimate means to an end. My dignity, my reputation, my independence and my pride are very important to me. I want to help other people; I want to feel I'm making a social contribution. When I consider these objectives, a successful career has been the way for me to accomplish these goals.

B.7: LIFE IS LIKE A MARATHON

Everyone leaves the starting line together. Some tear out in front, only to burn out early. Others are poorly conditioned and unprepared to last longer. They drop out, too.

Finishing first is important only for a few. Being able to finish at all is the objective of most.

Winners pace themselves. They know their capacity and they are prepared. They do not run too fast for their condition, nor do they run too slow. They are not concerned with how other runners are performing. They want to prove their own capacity.

As in marathons, to excel at our careers we must learn to run against the clock and our own performance to assure victory. Each of us must develop day by day, improving our stamina by the month and year instead of sprinting by the day and week.

It's easy to be overwhelmed by numerous tasks, especially ones with which we are not familiar. It can be confusing and demoralizing. Even if the initial excitement and intensity result in dramatic short-term results, over the long haul our enthusiasm will be worn down. The impressive short-term record will collapse into a frustrating confusion. Short-spurt heroes are not uncommon in life, but long-term, mature successes are rare.

If we work at our pace, have patience and a positive mental attitude, long-term success is guaranteed.

B.8: WINNING ENVIRONMENT

Personal appearance is very important in making a strong first impression. However, it takes more than good grooming to make a winner. There are many things that contribute to our overall impact: our home, office and automobile, to name a few. I am not suggesting that you've got to have a Rolls or a designer-decorated office to communicate success.

Think about a real estate agent taking a client to see a house in a car filled with litter: empty cans, bottles, food packages, cigarette packs, papers, old clothing. Not very appetizing is it?

Sometimes those littered cars are new and expensive. Yet I've been in older model cars that are clean and lovingly maintained. I get a far more favorable impression from the driver of the clean car. Wouldn't you?

It's also possible that an overly expensive car, home or office can intimidate some potential customers. You want to buy a home and your maximum budget is in the $100,000 range. If the real estate agent drives up in a Ferrari, your immediate reaction might be that this person is out of your league.

On the other hand, in an upscale, high-income market, that might be interpreted as a sign of success. Therefore, we are not talking about the material value so much as we are talking about the way it is perceived.

Likewise, some offices are in shambles with broken furniture, papers and old coffee cups scattered over the desks, counter tops, window sills and the floor. The paint is chipped and there are no wall decorations. Offices like these give a negative impression. We must pay attention to the environment created. Try to see your world through the eyes of others. In other words, clean up your act if this section applies.

Winners act and live like winners. The message is delivered by everything we do and everything we own. That's why CEOs

have executive suites. They symbolize success and communicate a positive message to all visitors. You are your own CEO.
Act accordingly.

B.9: PEOPLE POWER

Stars in every profession leave their footsteps in the sands of time (or the Walk of Fame!), but you don't have to be famous to have an impact on others. Most people with this special power don't even know they have it.

We begin our careers feeling average or inadequate. As we gain capacity and strength, the change is so subtle we usually underestimate the influence we have on the lives we touch.

An example comes from my wife, Sandy. She volunteers at the Children's Hospital at Stanford in California. Joey was 10 years old when he began a treatment program to cure his cancer. During that period Sandy learned he was a baseball fan. His number one hero was a ballplayer who is now retired. By coincidence, that player is a neighbor whom we know personally.

Sandy got Joey some souvenirs from his baseball hero which thrilled Joey. But his real dream was to personally meet his idol.

On his last visit to Stanford Children's Hospital, Joey's young life was nearly up. Sandy explained the situation to the ballplayer. He agreed to meet Joey. When he and Sandy arrived, Joey was comatose. His family was on death watch.

Joey somehow opened his eyes and recognized the ballplayer. He forced himself into a sitting position and grabbed the hand of his hero. The ballplayer sat on the side of his bed, holding Joey's hand, talking. As it turned out, Joey was two days away from death. For the first time in days, he was sitting, talking and smiling with his hero. This was the greatest gift anyone could have given the boy.

On the way home, Sandy turned to Joey's hero and said, "Do you realize how powerful you are? You were the only one who could bring Joey out of his comatose situation. He had the greatest 15 minutes of his life."

The ballplayer said, "I don't think I'm anything special. I'm just me."

This may be an extreme example of people power, but it's not that unusual. Power people don't realize their potency. We may not realize it but we impact the lives of everyone we meet. We can contribute to their happiness, success and well-being. If we can learn to use that power to make the world a better place, we can become extraordinarily successful human beings.

B.10: SALES CAMPAIGNS

Most companies run sales campaigns to motivate their people to new heights. They usually select a traditionally productive time of year, or conversely a time when business is particularly bad, and try to pump up activity. Companies usually tie campaigns to incentives, recognition and rewards. Occasionally they will improve the product or reduce the price. It's a great time for a salesperson to capitalize on the opportunity.

Some people do extraordinarily well during campaigns, others don't. The latter group justifies their attitude by saying, "I don't believe in campaigns. I do the same thing all year round so I don't need this for motivation." Some do have consistent sales records to justify their position. However, others are, at best, mediocre. They make excuses to avoid being competitive, stressed or embarrassed by their potentially poor production.

Some people rationalize that campaigns are for the sole benefit of the company. Sure, it's good for the company to do more business. It's also good for the employees.

Increased compensation, ego recognition and incentive rewards, such as gifts or conventions, are all part of every sales contest. Who benefits when the adrenaline flows?

When you get caught up in a sales contest, you find energy and enthusiasm that has been held in check. A camaraderie and synergy develops as people get caught up trying to outperform their greatest previous efforts. In each of our worlds there are special times that are opportunities to participate in a group effort that can add fun and motivation to our lives.

We should each accept these challenges and commit to greater achievements. Amazingly, once people have reached a new height, the bar is raised for the future.

B.11: INDUSTRY AND COMMUNITY PARTICIPATION

Volunteer work, educational participation, meetings and conventions can be inconvenient—even boring. However, one price of great success is some level of participation in one or all of the above. Winners are joiners and activists, in and out of their professional worlds. They will occasionally be with people and in situations not to their liking. On the other hand, they meet contacts who will become friends, confidants, mentors and role models.

Synergy compounds our effectiveness every day of our personal and business life. In theory, if you add the production of one person to another person you should only get the output of two people. In reality, two motivated, compatible people will almost always produce more than two people would have alone —the effect of synergy. Conversely, two negative people will drag each other down and will produce significantly less than they would have alone.

Synergy impacts all interpersonal relationships. I have never been to any meeting, even the very worst, when I didn't come away with at least one new acquaintance, one new idea or some skill which I incorporated into my daily living. The bad information, boredom or negativism is soon forgotten. The good things become a permanent resource and asset.

It's the combination of all the people, experiences and ideas that will accelerate your personal growth and achievements. If you don't participate you will lose great opportunities for friendship, love and assistance. You will lose the extraordinary sensation of sharing your own special gifts with others.

B.12: EDUCATION

Far too many people who thought their education was behind them are having a difficult time keeping up. There are many educational sources available. Most of us have in-company education and training programs. It is always appropriate to review the basics, as well as learn about new and more sophisticated technologies. All of us have forgotten more than we will ever remember.

Other available opportunities include industry-wide specialized education and training. Some careers have academic designations to identify those practitioners who have taken the time to educate themselves above and beyond the masses.

Pension planners and people who sell real estate, life insurance, and property and casualty insurance, as well as doctors, dentists, teachers, administrators, architects, interior designers and so on, have degrees that communicate academic excellence.

Industry and privately sponsored sales and motivational meetings and home-study courses are all valuable sources of information. There are unlimited periodicals, tape cassettes and videos.

One thing is certain. Keeping up requires constant exposure to the techniques and factual changes occurring on a daily basis. Many industries have professional associations for practitioners. If yours does, take advantage of their education and training activities. In these hectic evolutionary times, we can't depend on yesterday's knowledge to solve today's problems.

B.13: WE AND THEY

There are many stressful issues between management and their employees or field representatives in most industries; issues such as loyalty, compensation, contracts and competition.

Need it be so? I don't think so. It would take more space than this book to fully explain what it takes to create a suitable environment. Here are some essentials:

- Loyalty should be expected from both parties.
- Commitment to a common cause creates high morale.
- Communication is essential and is a two-way street.
- The system must reward participants, both monetarily and nonmaterially.
- Losers and time-wasters must be eliminated.
- Alternate intra-company systems can reinforce production and efficiency.
- All individuals and all divisions should strive to be compatible and cooperative with each other.
- All company divisions and subsidiaries should cooperate with each other.
- There can be no apparent favoritism within a company.
- Products and compensation must be perceived as fair.
- Employees should respond with commensurate productivity and company support.

There is no doubt that in such a healthy, successful environment, everyone will benefit from high morale. The result will be increased production.

B.14: 24-HOUR PERSON

The most successful people I know work seven days a week—even when they are playing.

Too many people work only during working hours. Of 80 potential work hours, they put in 40, at most (that's not counting time at the water cooler, long lunches, gabbing, talking on the phone to friends and family). These so-called producers would do better if they got their act together and concentrated on their chosen business identity.

This is true for everybody but is especially true for salespeople. Often their target market and their social life run concurrently. You can sell an insurance policy on the golf course or a handball court. By being ready 100 percent of the time, you can increase sales opportunities, expand comfort zones and enhance effectiveness. If a salesperson were to work and play in the same environment, the opportunity would be greater than if the exposure were limited to an 8- or 10-hour work day spent with target prospects.

Adjusting to this 24-hour concept is often inconvenient. It feels as though work is intruding on everything you do. Take it from one who knows. Eventually it not only becomes comfortable, it becomes fun.

The pecking order dominance necessary to improve interrelationships with top executives and better markets increases as upscale people become social friends. To achieve this desirable status a plan of approach might include the following:

1. Determine your target for types of relationships.
2. Identify areas, activities, special interests and hobbies where those people congregate.
3. Move to a more appropriate neighborhood.

4. Join groups and organizations dedicated to those identified activities.

5. Develop similar identified interests in those areas you
find interesting.

6. Dress appropriately for work and play.

7. Become an active participant and/or leader in the area
you chose.

8. Entertain people you meet in this new world.

Although this may sound difficult and expensive, it needn't
be. Pace your efforts. In time you can increase the speed of the
transformation and the money expended to suit your personal
situation.

B.15: PROFESSIONALISM

In every persuasion—doctors, lawyers, accountants, politicians, salespeople—there are peddlers and there are professionals. Unfortunately, the peddlers make the headlines. High ethics and honest morality are not a monopoly of any profession. In each persuasion, as in all things, there are some good and some bad.

The marks of a professional are: integrity, care, knowledge, service, skills, empathy, honesty and compassion. Without those attributes we are peddlers or worse. Frank Bettger said, "You have to act it to be it."

My dad was a physician, a career that everyone accepts as a highly ethical profession. He was also a great father and encouraged anything I aspired to in my youth. I left home at a young age, went to college, then tried many different things: boxing, bartending, farming. As I embarked on each of these short-term careers, Dad would say, "Just be the best you can be."

In 1948 I became a life insurance salesman. For the first time I noticed my dad was disturbed. He finally mustered the strength to say, "Be the best you can be, Son. And don't worry about college for your kids. I'll pay for it."

That hurt, but I knew the reason. Public perception of life insurance salespeople was that they were peddlers. I became quite successful at my chosen calling. When my dad had a heart attack I couldn't accept that this giant, whom I loved and respected, was experiencing the human frailties of old age and illness.

Then, during a hospital visit he gave me the greatest gift I have ever received. He reached over, took my hand, smiled, and said, "Norman, if I had my life to live over again, I'd be a life insurance salesman just like you." I'm forever grateful that he had a chance to tell me that.

I knew he loved me. What I didn't know was that his perception of life insurance salespeople had changed. As Dad watched me mature and succeed, as he met my peers and attended some sales meetings, he saw the other side—the professional side.

Since perception is reality, how are you perceived by your audience or clients? If it's not as a professional, change. Perception is everything. My dad's story is proof.

ACTION PROJECT

Comfortable Networking

1. Identify those markets which would represent quality future potential and which you would currently find comfortable for your own personal pursuit/interest.

CATEGORIES

Industries or Professions   _____

Business Enterprises   _____

Trade Associations   _____

Sporting Activities   _____

Community Activities   _____

Homeowner Associations   _____

Political Groups   _____

Charitable Organizations   _____

Religious Groups   _____

Ethnic Groups   _____

Family Clubs   _____

The Arts   _____

Science   _____

Other   _____

2. From among the above, select only those that have a strong personal interest and appeal.

Look at each of those groups and determine which of them are large enough to justify your time and energy.

From those groups, which ones are most likely to consist of many individuals that are qualified potential relationships or prospects?

List them here: _____ , _____ ,

_____ , _____ .

3. In each of those identified groups who are the most influential people you know and can personally approach?

Group: Influential people:

_____   _____

_____   _____

_____   _____

_____   _____

From among the remaining list select one or two you will pursue.

4. Plan a long-term program to cultivate these target groups as a permanent potential market source.

Start by asking your "influential" contact to accompany you to your first meeting and introduce you around to some key people.

Then consider:

A. Using directories and rosters to help identify and meet other members (not to initially solicit).
B. Developing centers of influence from among the identified influential people.
C. Advertising in group's magazines and periodicals.
D. Inviting key people for dinner or other social opportunities.
E. Volunteering.
F. Contributing to a charity or organization.
G. Helping or initiating the creation of a new formal organization (if none currently exists).
H. Asking present personal contacts for referrals to key leaders in identified areas.
I. Exhibiting at meetings, conferences or conventions.
J. Speaking at local, regional or national meetings.
K. Writing articles on your expertise for group publications.
L. Directing mail programs to other members.

M. Sending newsletters or a regular monthly letter to desirable contacts.

N. Sponsoring seminars.

Letters A through K are activities which must appear to be purely motivated by your interest in the purposes of the organization and not a business self-interest. These should be your only activities until you are firmly established in the group. Letters L, M and N should not be "actively pursued" until you earn the right and on a selective basis.

5. If you are a professional salesperson, allocate time each week to pursue the chosen groups.

A. Spend no more than 20 percent of your total potential selling time.

B. Continue doing what you have been doing that's been working in other market areas until results from target markets justify a reallocation of time.

C. Keep records to determine which sources and activities produce profitable business.

D. Work on these identified activities for at least six months (a year would be better) before abandoning them or making a major time and resource investment in any one area of activity. The final decision should be based on objective result analysis, not instinctive reactions.

Good hunting, and have fun!

3

Well-Being

C.1: AN OVERVIEW

Stories about intense, highly successful people suddenly passing away are not unfamiliar. Constant pressures to give above and beyond the call of duty extract a high price from your physical and mental well-being.

While there are no guarantees, changing your tension-filled lifestyle can increase potential longevity.

Too many people react to warnings about poor eating habits, stress and long work hours with a bravado that often seems inappropriate.

A typical statement is: "I'll get my exercise being a pallbearer at the funeral of my friends who exercise." That's tempting fate.

Hard-charging, competitive people must change their attitudes to improve their mental and physical health. They must try harder. We should all try:

- To watch our diets.
- Not to smoke.
- To exercise properly.

- To have regular checkups.
- To avoid stress and anger.
- To avoid excess alcohol, pills and stimulants.
- To avoid overwork and strenuous play.

Being optimistic and positive, taking vacation breaks, watching our weight and blood pressure, all help keep our human machines running well.

More importantly, learn to control time; don't let time control you. Time pressure is a major contributor to stress which is one of the main causes of cardiovascular disease.

Take care of yourself; it's a matter of life and death.

C.2: PAPER, TIME PRESSURE AND STRESS

Tension and stress impact heart disease. Hypertensive people are Type A. This group is more susceptible to heart disease. One of the contributing factors is trying to do too much in too little time. (See L.14 in chapter 11.)

My habit was to attack my paperwork either early in the morning or toward the end of the day, when interruptions were at a minimum. Unfortunately, my time was limited. I had appointments in the morning; in the evening I was expected home for dinner. Cleaning up piles of paper when rushed by the clock is a great tension creator. To reduce stress I now clear two evenings a week then dig into the paperwork without time pressures. I probably have more paperwork than most but I can get it all done in these two open-ended evenings.

I make To Do lists, which I carry at all times. I use time in my car to return calls. When my desk is clear I am ready for a fresh start. This procedure significantly improves my effectiveness and eliminates most time-related stress.

Try it, you may like it.

C.3: STRESS AND THE UNDERACHIEVER

There is "good" stress and "bad" stress. The former makes you feel up, the latter makes you feel uptight.

Good stress improves performance. Bad stress will negatively impact performance and can ultimately kill you.

The overachiever who has not learned to say no takes on far too much work. The result is constant stress.

However, to suggest that underachievers slow down is counter-productive. There is even more pressure when a person fails to achieve his minimum expectations. Failure is one of the worst anxiety-makers.

If the workaholic must learn to say no and take time out to relax, the underachiever should set realistic targets and move toward those goals. He should be directed to a less stressful life through job satisfaction and ego rewards. Extremes are dangerous. We should all strive for a proper balance.

C.4: BUSINESS MENOPAUSE

Menopause, for lack of a better word, sets in when people have attained all or most of their goals. Once their objectives have been attained—money, recognition, creature comforts, acceptance—there appears to be nothing left and boredom begins.

At this point anything can happen—from quitting their career or their special interpersonal relationship, taking long sabbaticals, or simply accepting tedium as a way of life. The sad part is, it doesn't have to be that way. Some people remain excited, motivated, vital and productive forever. Just look at actress Jessica Tandy, author George Bernard Shaw and comedian George Burns.

If people kept adding new and interesting things to their life, the problem would disappear.

Most successful people genuinely like the challenge of their work. They care about their clients, associates, company and the community they serve. They hate to give up the whole gestalt of their industry, even when they should be thinking about retirement.

We often run away from or rationalize away the very things that would bring us happiness!

Even if menopause has set in, there are possible cures. The following list suggests activities that might also serve as preventive therapy if you are feeling burned out.

1. Dream big dreams and reaffirm what you really want from life.
2. Make new long-term and short-term goals.
3. Remain flexible; don't get into a rut.
4. Stay involved in your company's business even if you don't have to be. It's not what you get but what you can give back.

5. Attend industry-related functions; participate as a leader. Have fun.

6. Become involved in politics.

7. Help bring new people into the business. Be a Big Brother or Sister. It will stimulate you.

8. Become a mentor.

9. Accept new challenges.

10. Study regularly. Break into new, undiscovered territory.

11. Join a study group.

12. Seek public speaking opportunities, especially at schools or colleges.

13. Occasionally design or redesign your brochure, letterhead, proposals, office facility, etc.

14. Don't do things that bore you.

15. Create family time; plan vacations on a regular basis.

16. Develop one or more successful protégés.

17. If you have been swamped with organizational work, drop most of it. Use your new free time for you and your family.

18. Spend your time enjoying business and social relationships with people you really like.

19. Enjoy life.

C.5: RECREATION

Everybody must have time dedicated to recreation. A vacation should be a reward for achievement. No matter how strong an individual thinks he or she is, the body and mind can take just so much constant stress and pressure until it collapses.

It is a sound business practice to schedule five-day or longer holidays every three or four months, as well as a long, pleasurable weekend every month or so. Time should be allocated for family pleasure—a movie, the theater, bowling, playing with the kids, eating out or romantic evenings with your significant other every single week. It's good therapy and good for family relationships. These can easily be scheduled without taking away essential time for career development. Once scheduled, these activities should be absolutely sacred.

Life is a marathon, not a sprint. You don't have to win all the accolades in one year. That means pacing yourself. One of the best devices is having time-outs for rest, recreation, vacations and family.

One significant caution. To vacation and play without making sure you have rigid disciplines for your career development would be absolutely self-defeating. This concept should be a warning for those who might work too hard. It is also a warning that, if abused, it will accelerate the failure for those that don't work hard enough.

C.6: MARRIAGE ON THE ROCKS

High divorce rates are part of modern living. This, unfortunately, is a common problem in the arena of high intensity successes.

For example, it is not unusual for a salesperson to begin his career with reasonable intellectual, social and cultural compatibility with his spouse. They enjoy mutual friends and activities. They feel comfortable going to the same places, eating in the same restaurants. They enjoy the same friends.

Then along comes a totally new lifestyle. An immediate, intense educational experience begins. So does a new set of social contacts. There are new restaurants, fancy resort hotels, new clothing styles, challenges, interests, dreams and aspirations. Also during the early stages of the career, financial pressures may add to the family tension.

In this already strained environment, the salesperson is away from the family more and more. Normal communication may disintegrate. In time, success brings a greater income which leads to a higher lifestyle with new friends and social activities.

If this pattern continues and no attempt is made to involve the spouse, the total sociocultural gap between husband and wife can grow so wide and deep that marital tensions are inevitable. This scenario can apply to any business persuasion if one spouse is intensely involved in building a career and the other is left behind in their former world.

Although many business organizations care about involving the spouse, it is on a superficial level. This is not enough. Spouses should be encouraged to participate in educational opportunities, company and industry conventions, as well as recreational events. Children, too, when appropriate.

We often hear about children hating the parent being away so much of the time. Conversely, where good communications exist, children have followed in their parents' footsteps.

Communication with one's spouse is essential. Sharing ideas and business activities, and staying occupied productively will all contribute to more solid relationships.

Being a great business success can be a totally fulfilling family experience or it can lead to a marriage on the rocks. Complacency will not solve the problem. It requires effort that can affect the growth, success and happiness of any married couple.

C.7: FAMILY TIME

It's fun to be successful. But a full, happy life is a matter of keeping your priorities straight. Spending time with the family is essential.

When you take your last breath, it's highly unlikely that you'll be thinking about your career achievements, your golf handicap, your car or the trips you've taken. You will reflect about those you love and what you've done with your life that has made an impact on the lives of others. Of course at that point it's too late to change what has already been.

Regardless of your career ambitions, make sure your family and those you love are part of your everyday life. Smell the flowers, with your family at your side, as you travel down your career path.

From the time our children were young, they were included in our plans. If possible they came with us. They attended industry meetings, conventions—even academic sessions. They knew about our achievements and were also aware of our disappointments. At the time I didn't realize the impact those experiences were having on them. All three of our children chose to be in the same business I'm in and to live, with their families, within 15 minutes of our home.

Some years ago a vice president of a company told me he envied the fact that my entire family was with me at a company convention. He said he worked so hard his children resented his career. I believe my experience and his are a direct result of family communication and involvement.

I don't think there is any one particular way to build family relationships. However, there is no question you've got to find a way if you want your family around in later years. If you don't use this tip to be a successful whole person, then it is your loss.

ACTION PROJECT

Physical and Mental Well-Being

Your health and well-being should never be taken for granted. Though to some degree health is beyond our individual control, medical science has proven that the way we live can substantially contribute to our physical and mental wellness. Though a proper lifestyle doesn't guarantee good health, it does, on the average, significantly extend life. It also makes you feel better and, therefore, you can perform better.

To assist in this lifetime project, the following checklist can be used to rate yourself.

Major No-Nos	Problem?	
Smoking?	❏ Yes	❏ No
Excessive alcohol consumption?	❏ Yes	❏ No
Chemical dependency?	❏ Yes	❏ No
Overweight?	❏ Yes	❏ No
Cholesterol too high?	❏ Yes	❏ No
Too much fat intake?	❏ Yes	❏ No
Not enough fiber?	❏ Yes	❏ No
Too much salt?	❏ Yes	❏ No
Irregular eating habits?	❏ Yes	❏ No
Too much junk food?	❏ Yes	❏ No
Not enough sleep?	❏ Yes	❏ No
Irregular work hours?	❏ Yes	❏ No
Working too hard?	❏ Yes	❏ No
No regular exercise?	❏ Yes	❏ No
Stressed from lack of time control?	❏ Yes	❏ No
No annual medical checkups?	❏ Yes	❏ No

Major No-Nos   **Problem?**

Untreated medical problem?   ❏ Yes   ❏ No

High blood pressure?   ❏ Yes   ❏ No

Bad family health history?   ❏ Yes   ❏ No

Taking unprescribed medication?   ❏ Yes   ❏ No

No long restful weekends?   ❏ Yes   ❏ No

No planned vacations?   ❏ Yes   ❏ No

No weekly recreation time?   ❏ Yes   ❏ No

No nonbusiness interests?   ❏ Yes   ❏ No

Sometimes depressed?   ❏ Yes   ❏ No

Feeling great stress?   ❏ Yes   ❏ No

Not having fun?   ❏ Yes   ❏ No

Constantly negative?   ❏ Yes   ❏ No

Too many adversarial relationships?   ❏ Yes   ❏ No

Spending more money than making?   ❏ Yes   ❏ No

Not enough close personal relationships?   ❏ Yes   ❏ No

Not enough family time?   ❏ Yes   ❏ No

At every goal-setting and planning session this checklist should be reviewed. Every existing problem (yes answers) should be seriously considered and addressed.

Here's to your health and well-being!

4

Goals and Dreams

D.1: AN OVERVIEW

Ever hear the expression, "If you don't know where you are going, you will surely get there"?

Despite the acceptance of that premise—which suggests you must have a goal to which you are committed—I find most people do not have clearly identified goals.

Without the emotional commitment to a target, a driving force is rarely attained.

When emotional goals and business goals are the same, great achievements often follow. Often, however, they can be counter-productive to each other. Counter-productive emotional goals might include:

- Starting the day late.
- Ending it early.
- Sleeping a lot.
- Taking Friday afternoons off.
- Taking long weekends.

While these are wonderful wishes, they are not consistent with great success.

Let me ask a simple question.

Where do you want to go and when do you want to arrive?

You have one life, a finite time to achieve your dreams. Don't waste it.

Dreams give the winners on this planet the strength to do what unsuccessful people won't do. Keep the dream visible and in focus all the time. Then convert the vision to long-term, specific goals. Break long-term goals into short-term ones. Once established, go for them. When you find yourself losing momentum, refresh and stimulate yourself by visualizing yourself being there.

The expression "pursuit of happiness" is only half right. Truly successful people have found the real expression should be "happiness of pursuit."

D.2: CHASING INFINITY

One key to staying motivated and excited is using short-term goals as the means to the end.

Think about buying a puzzle. The challenge of piecing it together stimulates intense, short-term interest. Once the puzzle is complete, interest quickly wanes and it is soon forgotten.

To sustain attention in any project we must chase infinity. A challenging goal draws us onward. Dream the biggest dream you can imagine. If you get close, dream a bigger dream.

For most successful people the problem is life is too short. Too many mountains to climb, not enough time. However, they live and enjoy every day.

Do you?

D.3: DREAM BIG DREAMS

In goal-setting, most people accept a comfortable level of activity: the hours they work, the people with whom they interact, the pace they have set for themselves. In other words, they continue to do what they have been doing, week after week, year after year.

Classically, that attitude leads to mediocrity. Big-time achievers are not looking for a safe zone; they have the courage to take risks. They visualize themselves in a year, in 5 years, in 10. They imagine their improved lifestyle, standard of living, level of success, self-esteem and ego fulfillment. Then they commit to getting there. No change, no gain.

People tend to get into a rut. They don't realize they are playing it safe. They're okay with where they are. While they could have a larger home, a nicer car, more exciting vacations, they have resigned themselves to accepting what they already have.

Ask yourself, "Is this all there is? Is this the way it has to be?"

Outstanding achievers say, "No, I can be anything I want to be. I'm prepared to pay the price to get there."

It's much better to be on the ballfield as a major leaguer, even on a losing team, than to be sitting in the grandstand and watching life go by. Major league players dream big dreams and great players are not afraid to reach beyond their comfort zone—even if it means losing a game now and then.

Too many people assume the super achievers in their field are gifted. They think ordinary people like themselves can't reach the same heights. Wrong!

Everyone starts out even. Apply yourself, take some risks and accept rejection as part of the game. Spend your time dwelling on your successes, not the failures.

Celebrate your victories and you will surely prosper.

D.4: COMFORTABLE PRIORITIES

Why do some people with great natural aptitude never attain more than average achievements?

From birth, people establish priorities that dictate their overall performance throughout their life. Think about the masses as compared to the superstars.

Priorities exist in the subconscious and are not always obvious to the individual. Comfortable priorities usually lead to mediocrity.

Simply put, most people prefer to goof off, to cut corners, to find the easy way. They avoid unpleasant yet essential disciplines. As human beings that does not make them bad or lazy, it just means they are average. However, it takes above-average performance to excel.

Like diets, the results don't last unless we change our everyday eating habits. Without total modification, the weight goes right back on.

People who are driven by disciplined priorities are usually happier working hard than nonachievers are goofing off. It reinforces the point that successful people will do the things unsuccessful people won't do.

To change comfortable priorities to preferred priorities is difficult. It may seem downright impossible. It can, however, be done by anyone who wants the results badly enough.

Concentrate and reinforce priority desires until the subconscious priorities shift. You should consider:

1. The desire for self-respect and ego-gratification that accompanies achievement.
2. The shame of being seen as a nonperformer by family, friends and peers.
3. The boredom and frustration that accompanies goofing off.

4. The coveting of the better things in life.

5. The desire for approval.

The key is wanting what is not easily available. If the desires provide a reward, you will eventually shift from comfortable priorities to achieving priorities.

D.5: GOAL-JOGGERS

On January 1, many people sit down and make goals, which they break down by the month, the week and day. Then they put the goals in a drawer and forget them. Aspirations are useless unless you give them your full dedication.

I've found a simple trick. I call them goal-joggers. On three-by-five index cards write a list of capsule goals (five words or less). The goals and cards can be shuffled from time to time. The best disciplined people I know take out their goal cards every day and review them.

Airline pilots, even though they have been through the process innumerable times, are required to fill out a written pre-flight checklist before they take off. What if they left without fuel? Remember, we forget more than we remember.

Although you may have memorized your goal-joggers, review the cards at least once a day to know where you're going and how you plan to get there.

D.6: THE PSYCHIATRIST

Many people blame their lack of success on what they perceive to be personal obstacles to their growth and development. They blame everyone and everything. They wear their problems like a badge and use them as an excuse for failure. Some enlist the services of a coach or analyst to help address the problem. Unfortunately, most of them never change and never become successful.

Often they themselves are the cause and the effect. I learned this in college.

I was always a fast learner and could cram for almost any exam in a one-night session. I didn't like reading and rarely did homework. I'd cut classes and finally developed a guilty conscience because all of my college friends were working much harder than I was.

I decided there was something wrong with me and made an appointment with the school psychiatrist. When I got there, the doctor asked, "What's your problem?"

I said I felt I was a poor student because I preferred goofing off to working.

When he asked my grades and I said A-, he replied, "That doesn't sound like a problem."

He added that if I was happy, well-adjusted and successful, I didn't need a psychiatrist.

From an academic point of view I'm not sure he gave me the right answer. From a peace-of-mind and well-being point of view, he most certainly did.

Ought to, is not a strong motivator.

Want to, is.

Being out of sync and unhappy with where you are is a problem. But having fun and doing well certainly is not. There are many ways to succeed in life. We should all do what we *want,* not what we *ought* and not what we *should.*

We can't hide behind our weaknesses. Complaining about them or bragging will not evoke sympathy. Everyone has weak spots. Achievers find the courage to fix them.

If you *want* to be successful, don't find excuses for failure. Find ways to succeed. Don't expect a psychiatrist, counselor or coach to prescribe a magic pill to make it eas

D.7: RULE OF 72

If you divide the number 72 by the compound interest you earn on a sum of money, the resulting answer will indicate how many years it will be before the initial sum will double. For example, five percent compound interest will double one's initial investment in approximately 14.4 years.

Whatever the current trends are, costs will increase because of inflation. Using the same Rule of 72, if a loaf of bread costs a certain amount today, at a five percent inflation rate it will cost twice as much 15 years from now. The cost of living and the cost of doing business will also double over a period of time.

Therefore, income needs will also constantly increase to sustain current standards of living. Further, people must provide for old age, which means a significant surplus of income over expenses must be earned, saved and invested.

Too many people stop growing at a comfortable income level. Those plateaued achievers will pay a big price for ignoring the Rule of 72. It is not unreasonable to plan for a doubling of expenses just to stay even at least every 10 years. Part of that increase will be inflation and part will be an enhanced lifestyle. Further, at least an additional 20 percent of after-tax income should be put aside every year to provide a significant nest egg during one's productive years, to be used when earned income may disappear.

Used properly, the Rule of 72 will help plan and budget for your own lifestyle by compounding your savings, and it will help secure your retirement. If ignored, however, the unfriendly rule of compounding expenses can destroy all future financial planning.

ACTION PROJECT

Goals, Dreams, Aspirations

Self-motivated people don't need motivation. They need encouragement, opportunity and direction to achieve their productive goals.

For a marginally motivated person, a good mentor can maximize his or her effectiveness. Some who might never succeed alone can find success through the inspiration of a role model.

It is within our own power to find self-motivation. Winners have a dream. Your dreams and aspirations are the fuel that fire the motivation engine. That's why an emotional commitment is essential.

Many people think quantified goals such as money and promotions are the motivators that make people run. Those are really only part of the plan—the means to the end. The real driving force are the dreams that you want to have come true.

This action project may help you find a dream which will start you down the road to great success. This action project requires private time for introspection. It requires that you write down an appropriate narrative answer to each step of the process.

Step 1: Visualization

To determine your 20-year objective, try to visualize where you want your life to be.

1. What is your wildest long-term dream?
2. Whose lifestyle are you most impressed with?
3. Who do you envy?
4. Whose lifestyle would you like to emulate?

Step 2: The Big Dream

Visualization is the first step in creating a dream goal. Now describe in detail how you see yourself in 20 years.

Income: $_____

Wealth accumulation: $_____

How many homes? _____

Where? _____

How many cars? _____

Make and model? _____

Married?   ❏ Yes   ❏ No

Children?   ❏ Yes   ❏ No

How many? _____

Political involvement?   ❏ Yes   ❏ No

Organizational leader?   ❏ Yes   ❏ No

Country club member?   ❏ Yes   ❏ No

Vacations per year? _____

Destinations? _____

No dream is chiseled in stone. Spend time visualizing until you get an emotional commitment to be something significant.

Think of life as a road map. You can always change the route and end up anywhere you choose. You are always in control.

So, too, with dreams and aspirations. Each day you do nothing is a day lost forever. Dream any exciting dream and head in that direction. You almost certainly will adjust as time goes on but you will be progressing and growing every day.

Step 3: Starting Out

To begin the journey you need a one-year goal. Consider your lifetime dream and ask yourself what things in your current life do you want to change in the short term?

- Family situation
- Home
- Automobile
- Education

- Income/career
- Savings
- Work ethic
- Relationships
- Organizations (which ones? level of commitment?)
- Community activities

Write down your dream goals for the end of next year, including any of these items or other subjects you consider important. Then make a specific nonbusiness plan to achieve those short-term goals. Consider it a first step toward achieving your dream life.

To achieve these goals usually requires significant changes in habits, comfort levels and personality. These are the toughest areas to change. This is the area that separates winners from losers, and where future stars convert the dream/goal into fuel for performance.

The following subjects must be identified for change and then specific actions must be planned for immediate action.

Step 4: The Future

Family:
- Do I want my present situation in a year? If not, what should I do to change it?
- Am I spending enough time at home? If not, what should I do?

Home:
- Is this the home I want a year from now?
- If not, can I realistically move?
- Where do I want to move?

Automobile:
- Do I want to drive this car a year from now? If not, what do I want?
- Do I need an additional car?
- Should I lease or buy?

Education:
- Do I need a degree? If so, in what?
- Do I lack the formal knowledge to pursue part of my dream?

Relationships:
- Am I lonely?
- Do I want to expand my circle of friends?
- Do I have too many friends?

Organizations:
- Would special-interest groups help me?
- Are there activities I would like to pursue but haven't?
- Would I like more responsibility in the groups I participate in?

Make a business plan to achieve income and wealth-accumulation goals. Before you can make and implement a plan, you must establish goals so you know where you're going and why you are making the trip. Action assumes you are prepared to pay the emotional and financial price of doing what the plan requires. The power to accomplish those objectives comes from emotionally committing to the rewards that come from achieving the goals.

The following is a basic business sales format to establish the specific goals/objectives.

Step 5: One-Year Plan

1. Do a one-year budget based on your dream goal to determine how much income you'll need for:
   Living expenses
   Savings
   Taxes
   Business expenses

2. Now work on a one-year plan: Annual income required: $_____
   Income from nonbusiness sources: $_____
   Guaranteed salary: $_____

Commissions/royalties: $_____
Subtotal: $_____

If you work on a commission, freelance or nonsalary basis, you must remember that holidays, vacations and unproductive time is nonincome-generating time.

All of this is meant to guide your thinking process toward achieving your goals based on a scenario of dreams-can-come-true.

Now that your desires are on paper, let's see how you can plan to realize them.

5

Planning

E.1: AN OVERVIEW

Once goals are identified, a specific plan of action must be developed. Plans are always subject to change. Nevertheless, one must be developed. It must then be put into action. This discipline, sustained over a long period of time, is a critical element in the activity of all successful people.

E.2: COMFORT ZONES AND HOW
TO CONTROL THEM

If anyone doubts the existence of comfort zones, consider the feeling we get in old familiar situations: our homes, a favorite restaurant, with certain people. In unfamiliar situations there usually is a subtle stress level that causes discomfort and affects how we behave.

Some mysterious thermostat seems to turn people's performances on when they fall below their comfort zone.

Fortunately, the boundaries of a comfort zone can be raised with personal growth, a positive environment, affirmative mental attitude and self-directed goals.

Unfortunately, the comfort zone can be stagnant with negative thinking, bad environment and no goals.

It takes a strong, consistent effort to impact our comfort zones. Relating this to business is an important part of self-growth, as well as a key to leadership effectiveness.

I believe most so-called slumps are comfort zones for some people, and not a slump at all. Production is activated during some months. This trigger could be financial pressure, a possible promotion opportunity, whatever. Once the person over-achieves for a month or so, the comfort zone thermostat turns off and he or she returns to a normal level of production.

If a company is geared toward big fourth-quarter earnings, workers fight to raise their annual expectations. This period is often followed by a down time, which usually begins around Thanksgiving. It can extend until late spring or until the money runs out.

This need not be so. The mature worker exhibits year-round stability.

Here are 20 items which, if followed religiously, guarantee current success and a steady pattern of raising one's comfort zone.

1. Dream big dreams.
2. Set commensurate goals.
3. Write them down; burn them into your mind.
4. Make a plan; break it down by day, week, month and year.
5. Implement the plan.
6. Keep records.
7. Share all of this with a spouse, special friend, peer, manager or mentor; share constant updates on progress.
8. Spend time with winners.
9. Think positive thoughts.
10. Have enough new activity—such as sales starts per week —to achieve your minimum objectives.
11. Plan vacations well in advance and condition them on achievements.
12. Work productively until the day you leave for vacation.
13. Forget work while vacationing.
14. Have activity scheduled for the day you return.
15. Establish some upgraded material goals (car, house, vacation) and shop for them before you are ready to buy.
16. Brag about your victories, but be equally communicative about your disappointments and problems.
17. Volunteer to help; become a role model.
18. Invest in your business to upgrade your image (clothes, office appearance, secretary, equipment).
19. Take a leadership position in an industry, community or political organization.
20. Start acting upon your dream today and you will surely get there tomorrow.

E.3: NEW STARTS

Most people have cycles that result in repeating peaks and valleys. The difference in the pattern between ordinary mortals and the superstars is that the star makes each peak a little higher than the last and the valleys a little shallower.

The average or marginal person has erratic peaks at irregular intervals and the valleys bottom out with no production whatsoever. The average will produce mediocrity or failure by year's end.

It's like throwing a ball up a hill. If it isn't thrown hard enough to reach the top, it will roll back down. If the effort is intense enough, and it reaches even one inch over the top, it will continue forward on its own momentum.

Some people have difficulty handling more than one task at the same time. They become confused.

For example, selling is like an assembly line: The process begins with prospecting, contacting for interviews, fact-finding, devising a solution, closing, product delivery, service, then back again to prospecting. The stars do all those functions concurrently. The average producer tends to do only one of those tasks at a time. Hence there are prospecting times, closing times, etc. As a result, when they have concluded the cycle they are temporarily out of business until they pump up new activity and start all over again. This basic truth applies to all people in all endeavors.

The best and simplest technique I have developed to alleviate this problem is to presume that each of us will complete any important activity once it is started. Therefore, try to start new sales activity each week; the subsequent steps will be pursued automatically. The number of new starts is determined by calculating our personal needs to meet our production objectives. If rigidly maintained, constant growth is inevitable.

E.4: THE PRICE OF SUCCESS

There are no free rides to success. If there is something we really want, we must pay a price. Some things cost too much. We can refuse to buy them. Sometimes I'll buy something that I don't have an overpowering desire for because the price is right. On the other hand, there are things I want that I walk away from because they cost too much.

So it is with success and mediocrity and life's objectives.

If you pay a small price and avoid failure, you will only receive mediocrity in return. If you want more, the price is higher. You must reach a balance with which you are comfortable.

Some people who appear content would be more successful if there weren't a higher price to pay. Whether it's longer hours in the field or at the office, frequent business trips, weekends at their desk instead of on the golf course, they have decided that other things in life are more important.

An associate of mine worked seven days and seven nights a week. He was only unhappy when there wasn't someplace to run to; but that was his thing!

Frankly, it's not my thing. There is more in life than just making a lot of money. However, I couldn't live with myself if I weren't reaching high enough success levels to be respected by my peers. That's me!

How about you?

How badly do you want what you don't have?

How high a price are you prepared to pay?

Once those questions are answered, you should sit down and figure out how you will get the job done. Then do it.

E.5: WHAT IS FULL TIME?

Successful entrepreneurs work long hours with complete dedication. Their employees, however, are often content with a nine-to-five, five-day-a-week job, as long as there are adequate vacations and fringe benefits.

The store owner may put in a six-day, six-night week while risking a significant capital investment. The professional will spend many years on education and then open a practice at a great financial cost, and work long hours before enjoying the fruits of his labor.

A sales career has all the advantages of being in business for yourself at a minimal financial risk. But it demands hard work, commitment and dedication. The salesperson should be mentally prepared for at least a 60-hour work week, but unfortunately only a few are that intense.

Good salespeople can't tell when they are working or when they are playing. They are alert to career opportunities at all times. Friends are clients and clients are friends. A full-time salesperson is totally committed.

The successful person is also a good citizen and a family person. For that reason, it is absolutely essential that ample time is scheduled for home and community affairs. Nothing should interfere with those priorities.

It takes a talented person to keep all the balls in the air at the same time. The truly great ones make a significant contribution to the community; they are dedicated to their families; they are intense, committed professionals who are able to have fun, too.

E.6: BALLERINA'S COMMITMENT

Some time ago I saw an interview with the prima ballerina of the San Francisco Ballet. The host asked, "What is your favorite food?"

Much to my surprise she answered, "Ice cream sundaes."

"I didn't expect that answer," he said. "How often do you indulge?"

The ballerina's reply was a classic.

"Oh, I haven't had an ice cream sundae for at least 15 years. I knew if I wanted to be a prima ballerina I'd have to give them up. But they're still my favorite."

All great successes have priorities. For the ballerina, the sundaes had to go. Most aspiring successes, salespeople included, don't have to give up very much to succeed, but they do have to get their priorities straight. This often means lots of minor inconveniences. That is the price of prosperity.

As every successful person has found out, it's worth it.

E.7: THE PLAIN YELLOW PAD PROJECT

Many years ago I developed a technique which has helped me during slumps, times of frustration and times of re-evaluation.

I take a blank yellow pad to a private place and contemplate. As thoughts come to mind I write them on my pad.

- Things I like and don't like.
- Things I perceive to be strengths.
- Things I feel are my weaknesses.
- Dreams that I hope to attain.
- The parts of my career I enjoy.
- The parts I don't like.

There were times I literally filled the entire pad. At other times not even a page.

Upon review, I separated the important items from those that were just minutiae. Without exception, most of the negatives, when objectively reviewed, were relatively unimportant, but the positives were very meaningful.

I noticed a pattern of the strengths far exceeding the weaknesses, the fun and rewards far outshining the uncomfortable parts of my life. I realized that the dreams I really wanted could only be attained by pursuing my sales career. These retreats and my yellow pad have resulted in a total reaffirmation of my career decision.

I try to determine how I could have more fun, be more productive, achieve my lifetime goals. What were the things that could then be eliminated or delegated?

Every time I do this I am recharged.

When I share this process with others, I recommend that they show their notes to a spouse, a close associate or a mentor.

They should ask for an objective critique of their new goals. A confidant's perception of their situation usually reinforces their decisions and gives the process more substance and credibility. Further, the confidant then automatically becomes a monitor and conscience to help keep the person on track.

I can't guarantee that this technique will work for everybody, but it has helped many people.

We create our own slumps, moods and loss of direction, so it's logical that within ourselves we can find the strengths and the wherewithal to achieve our dreams. It is difficult to think clearly and objectively while stressed and while experiencing negative thoughts. The isolation, the introspection and the recording of the good and bad thoughts, helps filter out the illogical and emotional and identifies the substantive.

The human brain either controls us or we learn to utilize its power effectively. I have found this yellow pad project helps maximize my effectiveness by using my brain power. It may help you, too.

ACTION PROJECT

Planning Activity for Guaranteed Success

Most people say they want to be successful but they won't do the things it takes to prosper.

For this planning system we will presume that you want to establish a foolproof system to develop the habits that will assure world-class success.

Remember, the number one cause of failure is inadequate activity. For example, different sales positions require different degrees of prospecting and contacting intensity.

Some salespeople have specific prospects or territories that determine who they will see and when. This is a distinct advantage over salespeople who have no identified prospects, no specific identified market and no prearranged schedule provided to them. Other salespeople don't even see their prospects; contacts are made over the phone or through the mail.

However, all people should have a creative system, which includes a plan for the consistent and effective contacting of key people in their life. They should also have identified skills and techniques to develop a steady flow of potential prospects. For the great majority of salespeople, a system of prospecting, contacting and recordkeeping is essential.

Interpolate the following plans and systems to fit your situation. For the outside salesperson (whose portfolio might include products such as life insurance, property and casualty insurance, business machines, real estate, books and periodicals, home services and supplies), the system should work with minor adjustments. For others it can be a road map to redesign as necessary. For example, professionals building a practice, doctors, dentists, attorneys and accountants, business entrepreneurs, philanthropic and other organization leaders can certainly adapt this process to their situation.

A Sales Planning Procedure That Works

Pick the same time every week to plan future activity and record past results. At this planning session make notes of the preceding week: Record the number of sales interviews, fact sheets obtained, sales completed, new starts, money made, new prospects obtained.

Depending on your sales situation, also record the source of the prospects, the sales presentation used, in which interview the sale was consummated (1st, 2nd, 3rd) and any other relevant information to confirm that the time expended was justified by the results obtained.

This process should answer the following questions:

What prospect sources work best for me?

Which sales presentations are most effective for me?

Do I have enough activity to meet my goals?

What is my closing ratio and is it good enough?

Is my average size sale big enough?

Am I prospecting regularly and effectively?

Am I in the right market?

Am I spending too much time and too many interviews on poor prospects?

After reviewing the past week's record, do a planning session for future activity. Establish your plan by quantifying the necessary activities to reach your goals. For the unproven salesperson, in an entrepreneurial sales career, the following are realistic and attainable minimum goals:

Book three appointments a day, see at least two.

Dial the phone at least 40 times a day for appointments.

If you only have two booked appointments today dial 50 times.

If you only have one booked appointment today dial 60 times.

If there are no booked appointments today dial all day.

Get 25 booked appointments on the books for the next two or three weeks in advance if possible. This gives you the luxury of saying to a prospect, "I am too busy to see you until three weeks from now but I promised (name of the referrer) I'd call you."

Once you have decided on your personal absolute minimums, here is the weekly planning process. Prospects are people with whom you have first-person contact. Suspects are those with whom you do not have first-person contact—yet.

Preparation for Each Planning Session

- Have 1,000 pre-approach address labels to lists of qualified suspects.
- Have your client files accessible on your desk or in your computer.
- Have a follow-up system for contacting clients.
- Have your activity diary or planner open on the desk.
- Have current lists of newly developed prospects and perhaps highly qualified suspects readily accessible.

Here is the procedure in a simple worksheet format:

Activity Planning Procedure

Number of interviews necessary to
achieve goals for next week   A. _____

Number of interviews already scheduled   B. _____

Number of new sales process "starts"
necessary each week   _____

Number of new starts already scheduled   _____

Shortfall of interviews required to
attain next week's goals   A − B = C. _____

No matter how many interviews are already scheduled, you must also meet your new start goal. The following sources will get additional new start interviews.

- Number of referred leads available to call next week. At a 1:3 success ratio, number of interviews likely to be attained _____.

- Number of clients and/or past qualified prospects triggered by your follow-up system to be contacted now. At a 1:2 ratio, number of interviews likely to be attained _____.

- Total number of new start interviews likely to be attained from phone calls. D. _____

The ratios mentioned above are guesses, but each salesperson will determine his personal ratio by referring to actual past results.

If there are not enough "potential new start interviews" (D above) to achieve shortfall of interviews (C above), do the following:

- Mail 10 pre-approach letters for every interview shortfall. (Presuming all will be called and it will take 10 calls to get one appointment.)

    # of letters _____

- Organize all people to be called from all sources with name, address, phone numbers.

- Identify days next week for different geographical areas and do not make exceptions when you call for appointments. Stay in the same area all day long for time efficiency.

- When in a geographic area bring potential names with you of other clients and markets in that area to fill free time if you are stood up.

- Fill in your diary for next week with specific allocated times for:

      next week's planning session
      family
      recreation
      meetings
      study
      daily phone sessions
      already scheduled appointments

- Mark times for other possible sales interviews allowing at least one and a half hours per interview.

- Remember, breakfast and lunch each day represent 10 possible interviews per week. Use Saturdays and Sundays for both new sales activity and business planning, if necessary.

- Now get to work!

	MONDAY	TUESDAY	WEDNESDAY	THURSDAY	FRIDAY
8	Office	Breakfast with	Breakfast with	Breakfast with	Breakfast with
9	Meeting	John Doe	Mary Dunne	John Martin	Anne Vegas
10	✓	Phone Session			✓
11		Phone Session	Dennis Jones	Phone Session	
12	Lunch with	Lunch with	Lunch with	Lunch with	Lunch
1	Joe Smith	Frank Cole	Fred James	Ruth Frank	
2	✓	✓		✓	✓
3	✓	✓		✓	✓
4	✓		Continuing Educa-		
5			tion Class		
6					
7		Family	Bowling Night	Planning Session	Family
8	✓		Bowling Night	Planning Session	Family

There are 22 appointments or opportunities for appointments in this example. To make as yet unfilled appointment opportunities evident when calling to set interviews, they are identified with a tick (✓). These ticks can be color-coded for geographic differences and time efficiency.

6

Developing Relationships

F.1: AN OVERVIEW

The previous five chapters have been guidelines for success for anyone. This, and the following three chapters, are geared specifically toward business people with an emphasis on selling. However, even if you are not in the selling game, the sales techniques that follow are applicable to all interpersonal relationships and, therefore, would be worth reading. Remember, for most people, mixing self-esteem and interpersonal relationships is the recipe for happiness. These sales-related principles are applicable to all interpersonal relationships.

The number one activity contributing to great success and dismal failure is the number of quality prospects the salesperson sees on a regular basis.

Generally speaking, the higher the quality and affluence of the buyer—and the more income generated by the sale—the fewer number of prospects must be seen.

Conversely, smaller sales or less affluent buyers mean the salesperson must see more prospects.

The skill of the salesperson must also be factored into these equations. The poorer the closing ratio, the more prospects the salesperson has to see.

Simply stated, the number one factor contributing to success or failure is prospecting. Interestingly, there are many different techniques. Finding one or more that work for you is the key to success.

Most salespeople have access to the techniques necessary to achieve their prospecting objectives. However, the mind-set of the salesperson makes a direct impact on potential sales. Those who succeed do whatever it takes. Failures usually lack the courage and/or the discipline to prospect.

F.2: THE PSYCHE OF POOR PROSPECTING

Prospecting techniques include:

- Direct mail
- Personal observations
- Referred leads
- Cold canvass
- Social mobility
- Telemarketing
- Seminars

Some salespeople can do these effectively, others cannot. For the latter, the problem may be inadequate techniques or skills. But more often the real problem is ATTITUDE.

It boils down to courage.

Saying "I have no one to see" is an absurd excuse for failure.

"I have no one I feel comfortable seeing" is more on target.

Prospecting is an art and a talent. While it can be learned, often it is a natural instinct. If, in your case, after a sustained effort, you don't see enough people on a regular basis, your attention must be shifted to overcoming your fears. You must find your attitudinal blocks and change them. Or, you must find an alternate prospecting method to fit your personality.

You can do anything—if you want it badly enough. I won't lie, it takes courage, discipline, practice, patience and desire. These, combined with the correct mind-set, will lead to successful prospecting—and ultimately more lucrative sales.

F.3: TYPES OF PROSPECTS AND HOW TO USE THEM

There are many sources of prospects. For some salespeople prospects are provided or pre-identified. For others there are:

1. First-person contacts. These are usually the people you now know, or people you are exposed to socially or by networking with an organization or group.

2. Referred leads. These are people referred to you by a firsthand contact.

3. Qualified suspects. People you don't know personally but names you can identify as being the kind of person you are looking for. They may come from lists of employees, their business affiliations, club memberships, special interests, etc.

   The textbook definition of a qualified suspect is someone who can afford to pay, someone who can be seen under favorable circumstances and someone who has a need for the product or service you are selling.

4. Unqualified suspects. Strangers that can often be converted into qualified suspects. They may be as unselected as right out of the phone book.

   The methods used to find these prospects are as varied as there are salespeople in business. One well-known secret of successful people in sales is that they become experts in the methods of prospecting that best suit their personalities, products and services.

   If we were to draw a target, with the best quality in the center and the weakest outside, the bull's-eye would look like the illustration that follows.

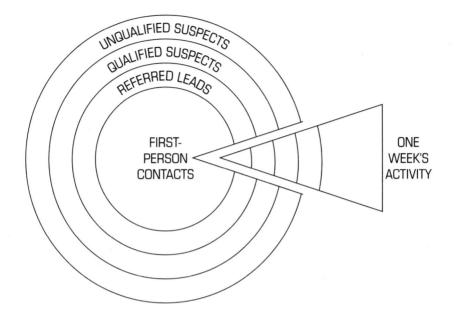

The new salesperson should cut a piece of that pie. The wedge-shaped slice would have first-person contacts, referred leads, qualified suspects and unqualified suspects. This could be a typical work week for a new salesperson who has not yet found the most effective method for selling.

Seeing various types of prospects early in one's career serves several valuable purposes:

- It doesn't use up all the best prospects too quickly.
- By spreading out the prospects it allows time to learn to sell effectively.
- It tests skills in all prospecting areas by finding the best personal sources.
- It gives a more realistic awareness of the salesperson's skill by not initially seeing only the most willing prospects.

F.4: QUALIFIED PROSPECTS

A qualified prospect:

- Can pay
- Can be seen
- Has need

As salespeople mature and succeed, their personal definition of a prospect often evolves into something like this:

Salespeople's Performance Level	The Minimal Prospect Qualifications They Look For
Poor Producers	Can see
Fair Producers	Can see, has need
Good Producers	Can pay, can see, has need
Superior Producers	Can pay, has need
Great Producers	Can pay

The pattern begins with struggling salespeople who will see anybody. Slowly they add other qualifications. When they get really good, they key on the potential size of the sale, i.e., the prospect's <u>financial</u> well-being. Eventually that's all they look for. Once a targeted prospect is identified, skill and persistence will eventually get an interview.

To reach that level, however, salespeople must survive in their career. This is done by having an adequate number of prospects and clients to see. To achieve that primary goal they should initially see anyone. Whenever possible, see better qualified prospects who can pay, be seen and have a need.

If you have time on your hands, activity is essential. After all, you never know when something may develop from nothing. Eventually, the nonbuyers will be weeded out and the prospects with the buying power will be targeted.

F.5: WHERE'S THE WHITE BALL?

A good pool player not only effectively makes the shot but sets the white cue ball in position for the next one.

Salespeople have the same challenge. Some put a great deal of time and energy into a particular prospect. Like the pool player, they must learn to position themselves for the next sale.

In this regard there are two post-sale opportunities which should be explored:

1. Is the customer likely to need additional products or services over a period of time. Cultivating interpersonal relationships helps maintain a favorable attitude for the future.

2. The second is to develop clients who not only buy your products and service, but also buy you. Such clients become a dependable source of future referred leads.

By positioning your activity for future opportunities when a sale is completed, you make a tough business easier. By failing to do this, you make difficult business even harder.

A good prospect with future needs, growth potential and a possible source of referrals is like a string of green lights in a staggered traffic light system. The first sale is only the beginning. Future sales are infinite.

As the pool player knows, don't just play the instant shot. Position yourself for the future.

F.6: YOUR TARGET MARKET

The purest form of target marketing is a pre-identified, limited group of people that can use the product or services you are selling or with whom you would enjoy an ongoing relationship. These selected markets can be approached by any one of the prospecting techniques mentioned elsewhere in this book.

There are also potential unidentified markets that are almost unlimited. Surprisingly, since this area is so vast, it is often more difficult for a salesperson to develop a substantial inventory of qualified prospects. It's like a kid with just enough money to buy one piece of candy. Where do you start?

Procrastination is also part of the problem. Outstanding sales-people are aware of this. To avoid it they concentrate on a few specific prospecting techniques. For those not yet so positioned, there are helpful hints for determining your most appropriate markets and prospecting methods.

Since no single mode works for everyone or for every market, here are some you may consider. They may help you determine which way you should direct your social and/or market activities.

1. Age: In certain situations a common age may help. Likewise, if a person is uncomfortable with people significantly older or younger, it could help determine an age group to be avoided or targeted.

2. Income: High-income people are usually better prospects for larger sales and also for upgrading your own social world. Yet some people are uncomfortable dealing with rich targets. Conversely, people can become impatient and/or domineering with low-income targets. Both attitudes should be considered in market and social planning.

3. Education: Sometimes the intellectual expectations or the

level of expertise required to socialize with, or sell a product or service to a particular person can make you feel inadequate. Only self-confidence can stimulate effective interrelationships. Therefore, knowledge and communication skills are a consideration.

4. Lifestyle: A contact's status and luxurious way of living can also create a feeling of inadequacy. The reverse can also be true. Selling downstream to people whose position makes you feel too superior can also be counterproductive.

   Many successes actually change their own clothing from day to day depending on the people they will be seeing. High-touch interpersonal relationships make for better selling. Some people are more adaptable than others, but certainly this criteria is a consideration when selecting a market.

5. Business resources: Some companies provide their salespeople with technical support, as well as material benefits such as cars and equipment. This allows the representative to address markets for which they might otherwise be unprepared. Available resources could be a consideration.

6. Products and services: Competition, price, servicing, location, delivery, advertising, public awareness and acceptance should be considered before targeting a potential market.

7. Social compatibility: Some of us are extroverts and some introverts; some dynamic and some analytical. To expect an introvert to be effective running seminars, cold canvassing or building a market on social mobility is unrealistic. Based on our own strengths and weaknesses, we each must decide where our marketing effectiveness is best used.

But don't misunderstand. Introverts can sell themselves at the right place and the right time to the right
people. As a matter of fact, some people would prefer
not to buy from an aggressive extrovert. The trick is finding where your personality can best fit the market you
choose to pursue.

8. Demographics: Depending on where you work, the
   makeup of the community in terms of race, color, creed,
   sex, affluence, etc., will influence your choice of market.
   It may even limit it completely. Sometimes adjustments
   must be made so you don't go on fool's errands.

These considerations should help you identify socially positive, desirable and profitable marketing opportunities, but they
are not all-inclusive. World-class salespeople have analyzed the
ones discussed above and added others. These additional considerations may have been determined by their actual experiences or by calculated decision-making.

All super salespeople eventually develop a comfortable, effective, productive, profitable market which they systematically and
aggressively pursue. They also determine which of the various
prospecting and contacting options discussed elsewhere in this
book are the best approaches to their identified markets.
Periodic reevaluation of their social life as well as their market
choice is part of their regular review and planning sessions
because things do not stay the same.

As we change, our products and services change, and the
markets we're addressing change, we must be adaptable
enough to stay at the cutting edge. Rarely does a person with
one group of friends in one geographic area—or in business in
one market with one approach—remain that way for an entire
career. Adaptability is the name of the game.

F.7: WOULD YOU MIND?

When a salesperson has established a comfortable social relationship with someone who also represents a great potential source of business, transitioning from social to business can be very uncomfortable, perhaps even frightening. Aspiring successes must learn to use these opportunities to build relationships, despite the discomfort.

Try taking this tack: "John, from what I know about you, I'm quite certain that the business I represent could be of great personal value to you. Would you mind getting together with me to discuss . . . ?"

The answer may be, "I wouldn't mind."

Or, "You're wasting your time."

Or, "I have somebody already helping me, but if you want to talk about it, why not?"

If the person shows reluctance, follow up with, "I can understand your position. I know this may not be the time or place, but I have something you might find of great value and you have nothing to lose by just talking. How about meeting for coffee next week?"

That sometimes opens the door. If neither approach works, I'd back off—but not before asking if I could mail them my newsletter. (See chapter 11, K.5 for more on this subject.)

The ability to convert social opportunities into potential business opportunities is a skill most world-class salespeople have mastered and one simple approach is asking with a nonthreatening, "Would you mind?"

F.8: UPGRADING YOUR MARKET

At some point in every sales career, it's time to upgrade the market. Sounds good doesn't it? But in practice it often leads to failure.

People usually have a social comfort zone. But the temptation of a bigger and more exciting market makes them strike out for greener pastures. When, and if, they attempt to work with more sophisticated contacts using their old interpersonal style, but with people with whom they are uncomfortable, disaster usually results.

Why does this happen?

They have gone outside their comfort zone.

The most effective way to move into the upscale markets is by evolution, not revolution. This is achieved by meeting new people through your proven comfort zones, by getting referrals or by using social mobility. The target is to move toward the new markets by meeting people with greater wealth or larger companies, while growing yourself through practice and self-improvement projects.

Though pay, see and need are the three hypothetical qualifications of a prospect, the primary criteria that most people use to determine an upscale prospect is wealth.

The dollar amounts may be bigger, but the interrelationship skills and techniques one must use are essentially the same. You must, however, be compatible and confident to implement them.

One very real caution. While this evolutionary upgrading is happening over a period of time, never stop doing what has worked up until that point. Eighty percent of each week's activity should be devoted to the comfortable activities that are proven successes with the current market. The remaining 20 percent should be trial-and-error efforts leading to ratcheting up your comfortable natural market.

F.9: PECKING ORDER

It is important that people understand the dynamics of upgrading.

There is a pecking order in all interpersonal relationships, just as in all animal relationships. A dominant attitude is established by one individual and subordinate positions are accepted by the others.

This is obvious to an observer by watching a salesperson enter a sales situation. The eyes, body language and attitude of the agent versus the prospect will determine who is in the dominant position.

Many people fail in developing desired social and business relationships by addressing markets or contacts where they are very likely to be placed in a subordinate position.

For example, some people are dominated by those older, richer, taller or better educated.

To attack the problem I strongly suggest that aspiring upgraders stay in relationships where they feel powerful enough to feel at least equality or dominance from the initial contact. This may mean deferring a lucrative market for the present. It doesn't, however, preclude calling in an experienced salesperson for joint effort on a split-case basis. As a matter of fact, joint interviews are one of the best learning experiences available.

Second, I suggest a personal growth program for them to raise their pecking-order relationships with others. This can be done by giving considerable attention to such confidence-building factors as education, dress, image, community status, home, neighborhood, clubs, hobbies, social activities, public speaking and political involvement.

Too many salespeople suddenly abandon a market in which they have been successful and make a major shift into another market where they are emotionally inadequate. The result is a career-threatening slump. If they upgraded by evolution—not revolution—while concurrently using associates who are "king chickens" for joint work, they will eventually grow into bigger markets and become king chickens themselves.

F.10: WHO KNOWS YOU?

Social mobility and networking are both effective sources of quality contacts. Even novice salespeople may become members of organizations surmising that the contacts they make will become a source of future business. Though the concept has credibility, a great deal depends on how effectively that activity is utilized.

In other words, it's not who the salesperson knows, but who knows the salesperson.

Would a new member point out the salesperson and say, "There's a power player"?

To be better known:

- You can't sit in the back of the room; you must sit in the front.

- You can't just watch what's happening; you've got to make things happen.

- You've got to invest time and perhaps some money in the organization to get the respect and recognition of your fellow members.

- You must participate in social activities and develop friendships with the power figures in the group.

- You should join a group, get known and have fun being there.

F.11: COLD CANVASS

When I was with the Fuller Brush Company, I literally rang a thousand or more doorbells a month. By using discipline and muscle, eventually I developed a reasonably good income. After a while I found this technique boring, exhausting and relatively low-paying.

The discipline of cold canvass is a good experience for any salesperson who needs the practice and discipline. However, over the long run I'm convinced that most salespeople should learn to work smarter, not harder. That eliminates cold canvass as a primary prospecting tool for many salespeople.

However, for those who might want to try cold canvassing, a review of the key points is appropriate.

- Be consistent and disciplined.
- Define the hours you plan to spend.
- Identify the locations.
- Rehearse the sales presentation to perfection.
- Learn to be resilient.
- Don't take rejection personally.
- Know that sales will come, based on the contacts made.

Cold canvass is a game of numbers. If you work 11 hours a day, you will earn 10 percent more than if you worked 10 hours. The more doorbells you ring, the more "no's" you will get. You will also get more "yes's."

The prospect's first impression of you has a heavy bearing on how effective you will be. Since you have only seconds to make your pitch, appearance, communication skills and the ability to open the conversation with "grabbing" information is critical. A successful technique develops over time.

When the door opens, the sales presentation must be powerful, brief and appropriate for the prospect. Asking a few questions early in the interview will frequently give you a clue as to where the interview should go. You don't have time to guess wrong and start again. Take your best shot as quickly as possible.

There are certain products and services that can best be distributed through cold canvass. Practice will sharpen your skills and eventually you will develop a profitable and effective method of prospecting.

F.12: RECOGNIZING REFERRED LEADS

Referred leads are the second best source of prospects. The first are people you already know. However, even the most sociable people need a larger pool of prospects. Qualified referred leads fill that bill.

A quality referred lead is a prospect who might have a need for your product and the ability to pay for it. So what makes a referred lead more valuable than some stranger with the same attributes?

The power that comes from the name of the referrer.

A power referral is one where the referral considers the referrer a mentor or authority symbol, and respects the referrer's judgment. That could include a relative, boss, valuable client, friend or organizational leader.

The more distant the referral, the weaker the value to the salesperson. If the distance is too great, the source's value diminishes to nothing. If the attitude of the referral to the referrer is negative, a phone book contact may be better since it's a neutral, not a negative, introduction.

Too many agents consider any name received from a referrer a referred lead. Technically that's correct, but only a power referral that is a qualified prospect has any real value.

F.13: GETTING REFERRED LEADS

Power-referred leads are a valuable source of business for salespeople.

There are only two reasons why someone will give a power lead.

- One is that the relationship to the salesperson is so strong that the referrer is not concerned with the possible outcome. The motive is to help the salesperson at any cost. These referrers are rare, and if a salesperson can cultivate just a few good ones they are doing very well. This type referrer is often considered a center of influence. Such centers of influence can be a close friend or relative of the salesperson or someone for whom the salesperson has done favors.

- The second is a desire to help the referral. These people may be, but are not limited to, the referrer's existing clients, friends, relatives, prospects and social contacts. If there is any doubt in the referrer's mind about the value to the referral, then names will not be given or will be of little value.

The techniques that are most effective in getting strong referrals include developing good interpersonal relationships with possible centers of influence and/or providing excellent service for the salesperson's existing clients, having good quality products at a fair price, superior knowledge of the product and business being sold and a sales technique that is perceived as professional and inoffensive.

Salespeople who wish to compound their growth and progress, and concurrently want to work smarter, not harder, must master the skill of developing quality referred leads.

F.14: DO ME A FAVOR

Many agents have a difficult time asking for prospects. They feel it's personally denigrating.

I totally disagree. All my prospecting techniques have improved since I developed a method that actually trades on my being comfortable asking for help.

My relationships with most people are strong enough so that they enjoy the opportunity to help me. People don't like to be subordinated. Conversely, they feel a sense of power when they can reach out and help somebody else.

So why not take advantage of other people's desire to help build your career?

The most powerful prospecting talk I have developed is this: "Mr. Prospect, I have a problem. Frankly, I really need your help. I appreciate your friendship, support and the business you've given me. The great majority of referrals I receive turn out to be a waste of both our time. Therefore, I'm going to try to spend time with people like yourself—successful, substantial, caring and sharing human beings—that are truly concerned about *their well-being* [fill in appropriate concern such as: their own personal problems, business problems, employee needs, customer requirements, etc.]."

I then ask that person to recommend anyone he or she knows that might benefit from my services.

Any variation of the above approach, adjusted to your own personality, product and circumstance, should result in a significant number of names.

Try it. You've got absolutely nothing to lose.

F.15: BE AWARE

Personal observation and capitalizing on those opportunities is a strong suit of most great salespeople. Many marginal salespeople walk by great opportunities and never even notice them.

Outstanding salespeople approach any potential prospect—with even the most remote opportunity—and eventually end up with some extraordinary stories of great sales. Regardless of the product or service you are selling, things are happening that could enhance your career all the time. Change in a potential prospect's business or personal life is often the perfect time for a salesperson to establish long-term relationships. Some steps you should take:

- Be aware of new businesses.
- Be alert to someone who moves to another business.
- Be alert to new franchise openings where you have sold to one or more other existing franchises.
- Note transfers or relocations within businesses or industries, particularly new people joining a business where you are well-known.
- Be aware of residential move-ins. If your products would fit a broad category of people, welcome new people to the neighborhood. It is always appreciated and can be a door-opener for future business.
- Make the initial contact sincere.
- Be aware of special occasions: graduations, marriages, new babies, new homes, new memberships in an organization.
- Watch for names in the news.
- Be alert to local happenings.
- Note happenings in trade publications.

These are all opportunities to make new contacts. Initially the approach should not be directly for selling, but the connection may contribute to your business growth.

Each of us has untold numbers of additional opportunities. What can you do to develop the discipline of personal observation and make it part of your daily and weekly activities?

F.16: DIRECT MAIL

Direct mail is usually a supplemental source of prospects. There are some businesses, however, that build their entire marketing plan on direct mail.

If an agent does not have enough people to see, a modest direct mail program to supplement the other prospect sources should be worth the effort.

The key to direct mail is maximizing the return on your investment of time and money. To be as effective as possible it makes sense to utilize proven concepts. Let me touch on several for your consideration.

Qualified Lists

The rate of return and the quality of the replier will greatly depend on the people who receive the letter in the first place. Anyone can buy a list or use a directory. But the more qualified the list, the more likely the results will justify the effort. Some of the things worth considering in developing qualified lists are:

1. Organizational Membership Lists: The return should be better if you share common interests with people from particular groups. Their very presence in those groups should make them potential prospects in your target market. Such mailing lists are worth developing.

2. Selected Businesses: If you are prospecting for certain business or industry-type prospects, lists are usually available from trade associations or printed directories. Nesting in specific business groups has proven effective for general product-type agents and might be essential for specialty-product salespeople.

3. Demographics: The career, age, educational level,

geographic location, wealth, income and interests are all considerations to consider. The closer the names on your list fit the type of person you're seeking as a prospect, the more appropriate your direct mail letter will be to their situation. The end result is effective sales.

Type of Mail

Salespeople tend to concentrate on three aggressively used methods of direct mail: pre-approach, reply mail and wave mailings.

1. Pre-Approach: This is a letter to attract the interest of the recipient and contains information that is general in nature. Pre-approach letters presume that the salesperson will call the recipients and attempt to set up sales appointments.

2. Reply Mail: These letters give more information than pre-approach but still leave unanswered questions in order to get the interest of the recipient. They often introduce items that communicate a sense of urgency. This type letter should be sent out in larger quantities. Anticipate that some recipients will reply. The letters sometimes offer gifts; at the very least they offer additional information. Have a reply card and an 800 number.

   This is most effective when sent by the multi-thousands over a long period of time. Expect a relatively low rate of return. Even less than a 1 percent reply may be acceptable. Depending on the product and the market, the numbers can be significantly higher or lower.

3. Wave Mailings: This approach presumes a series of mailings. Each one identifies the sender and discusses something new about the product and services. They are sent in sequence over several weeks or months. This method

presumes the recipient might not notice the first letter, but by the third or fourth letter they will become curious and perhaps will remember the name of the sender. Sometimes it helps to have a picture of the sender so a familiarity is established. After the third or fourth letter, the sender contacts the receiver in person or by phone. By referring to the letters, the salesperson hopes for a more favorable acceptance from the prospect and then attempts to get a personal interview.

Audio Business Cards

There are several firms that produce audio or video cassettes. The tapes describe the credentials, products and services you provide. It is a very upscale, high-cost approach. Most of the firms that manufacture these quality video or audio cards charge thousands of dollars for the initial order. They assist in creating the script, the audio/video materials, the cover letters, the design and the packaging. The mission is to represent the agent in a unique way.

In a few selected markets, this is an effective approach. However, I believe that without established credentials and without the perfect group of people to send the tapes to, most of these efforts do not justify the cost.

If you are just embarking on your first direct mail program, try two or three techniques concurrently. Keep track of the time expended, the effectiveness of the lists, the type of letters, the cost of the program, the need for additional sales activity and your sales results. Then you can determine whether or not you should continue a direct mail program. If you decide to continue, your research will also determine which of the programs might best suit your personality, products, services and expertise.

F.17: CREATING AND USING SPECIAL INTEREST GROUPS

If used properly, being involved with social organizations is a valuable use of time for anyone in sales. Even better is becoming a power player within an association, where you will become better known and recognized. The credit and recognition that comes from having been the initiator of such a group often spills over to other parts of community visibility, and increases your public respect and esteem.

There are several reasons for creating a group: if there is a vacuum in a specific area or if the existing organizations are not effective, have a frozen membership or are not an appropriate choice. Whatever the motive, if used correctly this is a valuable use of your time.

Some examples of these type groups are:

Tip clubs—Groups of professionals that meet for breakfast, lunch or cocktails to share concepts, sales ideas and leads.

Ethnic groups—If an agent is a member of a minority or ethnic group, it's a good idea to get a few key people together with the aim of uplifting, developing and enhancing that particular community. Referrals within the group are common and the interrelationships are invaluable.

Special interest groups—People with common interests (philanthropic, cultural, sports-minded, etc.) can develop local chapters of a larger state or national group or simply begin from scratch.

Industry groups—Organizations representing employees, executives and/or salespeople are not as common as they should be. While trade or self-help organizations exist, plenty of gaps still exist. This is a good opportunity to create such an organization in order to share business concepts and ideas.

Whether a new organization is created or one already exists, they represent a great valuable and pleasurable experience and a potential for sales. Most groups solicit advertising, they have conventions with vendor booths and need platform speakers. All of these are opportunities to promote products and services with dignity.

Some of the best salespeople I know that helped create new organizations were part of the founding committee and sat on the board of directors. This is practical because it takes less time to fulfill those functions than to be an officer. In addition, it's likely to mean a longer term of service at the executive level than if you become president for a year.

Another advantage to this approach is that it avoids political implications which can become fractional and competitive.

F.18: PROSPECTING DAYS

Most salespeople complain at one time or another that they have nobody to see. In most cases this is a by-product of call reluctance. It can also be the result of confused priorities. A salesperson must maintain a large inventory of high quality prospects. Sales activity must be directed at those markets. The whole system breaks down when there is no inventory.

Amazingly, agents who want to fix the problem can. In a relatively short time they develop a large pool of possible prospects.

To achieve this prospecting goal, salespeople should clear a few days every week to do nothing but build their prospect inventory. They should use the entire day to visit people they already know, and/or go to firms or organizations where they're already established, and/or schedule breakfast, lunch and dinner with some influential people from among their current acquaintances. Regardless of your product, interest or service, there are places where people you ought to know, but don't, gather. Go there.

These should be social calls, not sales pitches. During such visits request referred leads, qualified suspect lists (directories or employment rosters), or cultivate a few key people as possible long-term centers of influence.

Most people have the capacity to prospect; they just don't make it a high priority because they fear rejection. Who doesn't?

If you are favorably perceived by the people you call on, they usually enjoy the opportunity to help enhance your career. Really good friends may open their personal telephone book, go through it name by name and refer 50 names or more. When an organization or a business is visited, and there is a membership directory or roster of employees, visit a friendly key person in the firm. Ask that person to go through the directory and identify people you can contact using his or her name as a reference.

Incidentally, it's not a good idea to aggressively solicit large numbers of people from a single firm during business hours. The employer could be antagonized by that action and/or the human resource person might forbid any future visits.

Your own personal observation also helps you identify potential clients that you never noticed.

Eventually you will automatically recognize prospects who fit your target market. Make it a daily habit to seek such people by constantly getting qualified lists, referred leads and visiting centers of influence where you can get introductions.

Build your inventory and build your prospecting self-confidence at the same time. By incorporating all the appropriate prospecting ideas in this book, you should never again run out of prospects.

ACTION PROJECT

Prospecting

How to Get Started and Keep It Going

#1 reason for failure.

Salespeople must find a system/source that provides enough activity to achieve their goals. Some have a limited source of qualified prospects, others can approach almost anyone they meet. This project presumes anyone could be your prospect but each salesperson might have to apply these ideas to suit his own personal sales situation.

Possible sources: (See the concepts in this chapter for more detailed explanations of the systems and sources listed below and how to use them to sustain activity.)

Even experienced salespeople benefit from an occasional review of all the possible prospecting techniques to revitalize their current activity patterns. Check column one or two and then revisit these memory joggers whenever things slow down. Then also consider column three after two months of experience, to determine areas deserving increased attention.

(1) Already Doing or Not Appropriate	(2) Address Immediately	(3) After Two Months of Implementation List Top Three Resources for Your Sales
_____ **Current Personal Contacts** Often the best quality prospects available	_____	_____
_____ Relatives	_____	_____

(1)		(2)	(3)
_____	Friends	_____	_____
_____	Schoolmates	_____	_____
_____	Neighbors	_____	_____
_____	Former business associates	_____	_____
_____	Businesses you do business with	_____	_____
_____	Professionals you use	_____	_____
_____	Other: _____	_____	_____
_____	_____	_____	_____
_____	_____	_____	_____

Personal Observation

| _____ | | _____ | _____ |

This source plus referrals
and social mobility is often
considered the most effective
and productive.

Look for:

_____	New businesses	_____	_____
_____	Residential move-ins	_____	_____
_____	Marriages	_____	_____
_____	New babies	_____	_____
_____	Names in the news	_____	_____
_____	Other: _____	_____	_____
_____	_____	_____	_____
_____	_____	_____	_____

Referrals

| _____ | From people who want to help | _____ | _____ |

you (centers of influence)

(1)   **(2)**   **(3)**

_____ From people who want to help their referral (usually clients or attempted sales prospects)   _____   _____

_____ **Social Mobility**   _____   _____

(see Networking Action Project in Personal Attitude—chapter 2)

_____ Being active in social organizations   _____   _____

_____ Being active in service groups   _____   _____

_____ Entertaining others   _____   _____

_____ Community activity   _____   _____

_____ Charity or political activity   _____   _____

_____ Special interest groups   _____   _____

_____ Church and school activities   _____   _____

_____ Arts and sport activities   _____   _____

_____ Other: _____   _____   _____

_____ _____   _____   _____

_____ _____   _____   _____

_____ **Direct Mail**   _____   _____

This is generally used as a supplemental prospecting source but can, used properly and consistently, create a source of activity.

_____ Seek qualified suspects (lists to send mail to): organizations, demographic, geographic   _____   _____

(1)		(2)	(3)
_____	Pre-approach	_____	_____
_____	Reply mail	_____	_____
_____	Wave mailings	_____	_____
_____	Audio business cards	_____	_____

_____ **Seminars**

For a few select salespeople this
is a very dependable source if
the necessary skills and per-
sistency of effort are present.
(See chapter 7, "Contacting.")

| _____ | Qualified groups of suspects | _____ | _____ |
| _____ | Sponsored groups | _____ | _____ |

_____ **Cold Canvass**

Most experienced salespeople
eventually find this to be a draining
experience but for personalities
that can sustain high activity it can
work. Remember these points:

   Requires severe discipline

   Is a game of numbers

   First impression must be positive

   Must have a good, short, powerful presentation

_____ **Telephone Solicitation**

Unlike most prospecting techniques,
this is a method that can be delegated
to others. To be effective one must pay
attention to the following points:

Have qualified lists

Sole purpose of call is to get appointments
  (unless your product is sold over the phone)

Dial-and-smile technique essential

Requires skill and large numbers of contacts

Expect lots of "no's"

Practice, practice

You may not enjoy any of the listed sources or techniques. But to succeed as a salesperson you have no choice but to find prospecting methods that work for you. You may want to try all or at least many of them and then choose at least two, perhaps more, that are less onerous and more effective than the other sources, and keep doing them until they become an acceptable habit.

Suggested Process

1. Try each type of prospecting you feel is appropriate for you and your sales position. Identify the ones you plan to implement in column 2 of the checklist.

2. After a trial period, at least two months, analyze your results and then list in prioritized order the three techniques you found most comfortable that produced the greatest returns for effort expended.

3. Practice, refine and systemize the top three techniques and schedule them into your weekly activity plan by including them in your planning and telephone sessions, in your actual activity schedule, and in your recordkeeping methods. Be sure to keep records on your activities and results.

4. Periodically, when you do your planning for the future, reevaluate your prospecting procedures and review the list of techniques. Consider incorporating other techniques or eliminating those that are not then effective.

7

Contacting

G.1: AN OVERVIEW

Suppose the salesperson has developed the techniques necessary to achieve the right kind of prospects to sustain his business. The next potential roadblock to success is getting to see these potential clients under the most favorable conditions.

Once again, skill and courage are the attributes of outstanding sellers. Weaker salespeople look for ways of contacting prospects and making appointments using less effective, less stressful approaches. The degree of fear that the agent exhibits is sometimes described as the degree of "call reluctance."

There are many contacting approaches. The ones that capitalize on the salesperson's personality and ability are classically the most effective. For example, it takes a great deal more skill and courage to directly contact the prospect in person or on the phone than by letter. Direct, active contacting is a great deal more productive than a passive approach.

Poorer salespeople won't do the things necessary to acquire the quality prospects. When they do finally make contact they use less effective techniques.

Generally, the only reason for a contact is to make an appointment to start the sale process. But certain sales positions can sell over the phone. The common denominator of both approaches is nothing happens until some form of contact is made.

G.2: TELEPHONE SOLICITATION

Stockbrokers can effectively sell their product over the telephone. But for most salespeople, the telephone's primary purpose is to obtain an in-person interview. Every phone call should be powerful, brief and to the point. Since using the phone competently is so important, learning powerful phone skills is a high priority.

Developing the Skill: There are books, tapes and courses devoted to learning telephone solicitation. All of these can help accelerate your progress. Some people are more naturally gifted on the phone than others. Having worked with thousands of salespeople I'm convinced it's a skill that can be learned. It does, however, require a great deal of practice. All salespeople should allocate specific times every week, scheduled in advance, to be used exclusively for telephone solicitation. At these sessions, the only thought should be to get an appointment or, if your product can be sold over the phone, making a sale. Trying to sell a product while carrying on a social call is a waste of time.

To get an appointment, the person receiving the call should get the impression that you are a pleasant person; not adversarial or aggressive. In other words, dial and smile. A telephone sales track, crisply delivered and ending with a request for an appointment, is the ideal technique.

Finish each statement with an action question. For example: "Would you rather I come by Tuesday morning at 10:00 or Wednesday afternoon at 3:00?"

If the phone call lasts too long without moving toward an appointment, it's more efficient to hang up and make another phone call to someone else. If the prospect is dominating and is asking questions instead of answering them, the call is going the wrong way.

A good, crisp phone call introduces the caller, describes the company and type of work the individual does, suggests something that might be of great interest to the contact, and then suggests getting together so that the salesperson can show the contact something of great value or interest. The seller must communicate that the appointment is without cost or obligation, and will only take 15 minutes (or whatever is appropriate), unless the prospect asks for more time.

To most potential prospects, the things that are most likely to get them to make an appointment involve:

- Saving money
- Saving time
- Saving taxes
- Saving employee time
- Providing new business
- Increasing income
- Increasing comfort
- Increasing efficiency

Of those options you should select the ones most appropriate for your products/services and feature them in the phone call.

Perfecting this skill requires lots of practice and may take thousands of phone calls to reach a level of excellence.

Qualified Lists: The quality of the prospects initially contacted enhances the value of phone solicitation. If the person contacted is interested in the products or services you sell, you are more likely to get an interview. Then, when you see such a prospect, the probability of making a sale is greatly increased.

Developing the contact lists, therefore, deserves time and attention. Good referred leads, personal contacts, social contacts and qualified suspects are all better sources for telephone solicitation than just using the phone book or other nonqualified lists.

Game of Numbers: Even reasonably good telemarketers are satisfied with getting two good appointments for each hour of phone calling to an unqualified list. Since phone calls rarely take more than a couple of minutes, that means perhaps one call in 15 attempts results in an interview. However, agents with telephone expertise, contacting a very qualified list (perhaps referred leads), can sometimes get an appointment for every two calls. You must expect lots of rejection—certainly in your early career, since telephone solicitation is basically a game of numbers.

Remember, practice, even if it doesn't make perfect, certainly makes for higher levels of performance. If you dedicate time to the development of your telephone skills, your effectiveness in telephone solicitation will improve.

G.3: GETTING THE APPOINTMENT

How do you change prospects into interviews?

The answer is be relaxed and be yourself. The only sale you try to make when approaching a prospect is to sell the interview. Some sales interviews are conducted on the phone but even the first part of the phone call is "selling" the interview.

The salesperson must be in position to proceed with a sales effort. Whether on the phone, at a social occasion, or through cold canvass, you must ask in order to get the interview. Once you have accomplished that purpose, stop talking (unless you intend to make a sale on the phone).

The key is your tone: the way you think, the way you feel and your positive mental attitude. Always have a smile in your voice. When communication is contrived, our attempts are repulsed. Some salespeople are charming in nonsales-related relationships, yet they are cold and tight when they try to sell.

I am convinced many contacts are made by agents just to go through the motions. They salve their conscience while they "take a dive."

It's no big deal getting interviews; it's no big problem getting prospects. It's only a matter of courage and positive mental attitude; it's a game of numbers.

Over the years I have observed many marginal and failing salespeople who seemed embarrassed by their career choice. If we are not proud of the work we do we will never be good prospectors and contractors.

Converting prospects to interviews is often the broken link in the selling chain that leads to mediocrity or failure. Classically, this is called "call reluctance" which is really an unfounded fear that *must* be addressed.

G.4: PROSPECTING THROUGH SOCIAL CONTACTS

Salespeople who are socially active have a much better opportunity to develop quality sales than social hermits. Despite this obvious truth, there is no guarantee of profitable sales from social activity. As a matter of fact, while many salespeople have large groups of potential prospects, surprisingly few capitalize on them. When I ask why they don't pursue those opportunities, they either confess to call reluctance or admit to not knowing how to comfortably move a social situation into a business relationship.

Depending on your product or service, every person you know may not be a prospect for your portfolio. However, some will be. And all of them may know someone you might consider a prospect. Though there are skill techniques to help in opening those doors, the salesperson must:

1. Commit to wanting to pursue those people.
2. Discipline himself to do what must be done, call reluctance notwithstanding.
3. Learn and then practice the skills or techniques to accomplish the mission.

There is no question people known to the salesperson are usually better prospects than strangers. It is only fear that creates the false impression that they are not great prospects. Such salespeople would enthusiastically contact any referred lead from a near stranger while rationalizing the inadequacies of those they already know.

Two broad and basic techniques that have worked for me as an insurance salesman, which can easily be modified for any salesperson, are as follows:

1. The direct approach. Example: "John, I have known you for some time and have wondered if your financial situation will effectively achieve your personal goals. As you know, I am an expert in helping people plan and implement their financial well-being. Even if I only serve as a second opinion I would be most pleased to help you review your current position. Let's get together next week and discuss your situation."

2. For the more sensitive client, a gentler approach. Example: "John, we have been friends for quite a while. I'm sure you realize that I'm a recognized expert in helping people realize their financial dreams. Because of our friendship, I haven't been comfortable speaking to you about it sooner. However, it's important to make sure your affairs are properly in order so let's have lunch next week and talk about it."

Tailor the situation for your product or service.

Salespeople must take advantage of every opportunity. Find a way to use your social contacts effectively.

G.5: SELLING THROUGH SEMINARS

Having a group of potential prospects in one place at one time listening to your pitch sounds like an appealing way to approach the prospecting problem. If the presentation is done well, the attendees also benefit because they have a learning experience. They can then determine whether or not your particular products and/or services can be of value in their personal situation.

Though the idea sounds attractive, there are relatively few people who have successfully sold their products through seminars. There are many challenges involved in doing seminars effectively. Being aware of the potential problems will help you determine whether or not seminar selling is profitable. Here are some of the elements that can make seminar selling a waste of time or extraordinarily successful.

Developing the Audience

- General Audiences: To get a substantial audience, advertise either through direct mail, newspapers, radio or television. If the advertising materials are effective, if the market targeted is appropriate, and if the subject and/or products to be discussed are of interest, then this approach might be effective.

- Sponsored Seminars: Some companies, special interest organizations and general membership organizations will occasionally sponsor seminars that may be beneficial to their constituents. When this happens, the group is likely to be larger and more open-minded.

Location

- Geographic: Generally speaking, people do not like to be inconvenienced. Therefore, a geographically convenient location is desirable. During the working day it should be near your target market. On weekends or evenings it may be necessary to have more than one seminar at different locations to suit the convenience of those who are targeted.

- The Actual Venue: Having a reasonably well-known location, which has a reputation commensurate with the quality of the type of prospect you are targeting, makes good sense. Good lighting, comfortable seating, light refreshments and an upscale ambience all seem to contribute to the effectiveness of a seminar.

- In Your Office: Holding a seminar in your professional suite makes sense if it is easily located and geographically convenient. It helps if it conveys the impression you want to establish with your prospective attendees.

- In the Offices of the Sponsoring Organization: If the sponsoring organization will make space available and encourage participation, this is the least expensive, most effective way of developing an audience.

When to Hold the Seminar

- Number of Sessions: Seminars can be as brief as a teaser during a lunch break, or as comprehensive as multiple sessions. Both work. Only the salesperson can decide which is right for his circumstance. As a general rule we must decide effectiveness by the likelihood of converting an attendee into a prospect.

- Employer Sponsored: If the employer will allow the attendees to attend during working hours, that is the perfect timing. Since the location is convenient and a break is always appreciated, maximum attendance will be achieved. When it cannot be during working hours, the next best time would either be at a lunch break (with refreshments provided) or immediately preceding or following working hours.

- General Interest Groups: If the seminar solicitation is directed at home addresses it is difficult to predict the best timing and location. Experimenting with different locations, different times and different days of the week is an effective technique to determine what works best. Trial and error can eventually determine the best answer in each situation.

Pre-Meeting Arrangements

- Admission Fee: Some successful seminar conductors charge a substantial fee and provide valuable materials to the attendees. Some print tickets with a fee imprinted on the ticket but don't give away materials. They sometimes waive the fee as an inducement to attend. And still others take a free admission approach. All three approaches work and the specific circumstances will dictate which approach is right for each situation.

- Basic Arrangements: It is essential that there be an attendee response (RSVP) which is followed up with a phone call reminder just prior to the actual seminar. Some teaser information can be included in the "confirmation of attendance" to make attending very appealing.

  The meeting room should be completely set up at least one hour prior to the starting time, with a registration desk, light refreshments and handouts to keep the attention of those who come prior to the start of the meeting.

It is desirable to have one or more hosts or hostesses greeting each new person. Pads, pencils and kits of some kind should also be distributed, including a registration form to be filled out immediately along with a post-meeting critique form which also has space dedicated to setting up a one-on-one appointment subsequent to the seminar.

- Presenters: The primary motive for a seminar is usually to develop a prospect. Therefore, the seminars, though hopefully including significant substance, should not answer all the attendees' questions. The presentation should whet appetites in areas relevant to the kind of product or service being sold. The presenters, and there should be two or more, should make an attractive appearance. Good communication requires both verbal and visual skills so slides, easels or audio/visual support are advantageous.

  The presenters must have good stage presence. The salespersons, who will conduct the post-seminar individual appointments, should be featured presenters. There should be time for questions, but not so much that someone in the audience can start a debate. Attendees can't be allowed to take so much time that the rest of the audience becomes restless. They shouldn't challenge the presenter.

  To control the length and number of questions, the presenter can offer to answer individual queries at the end of the session in private. Or better yet, make an appointment.

- Materials: The actual materials can be purchased in complete packages from seminar promotion organizations. Some of them are quite expensive, others are reasonable.

Everything is available—mailing pieces, handout materials, scripts, slides, a training course and outlines, with or without slides. It would be prudent for each salesperson considering seminar selling to review the variety of materials available and the cost before proceeding.

Some of you may conclude that you are qualified and prepared to construct your own seminar procedure. Others might choose to buy complete packages. Both approaches work. If seminar selling is simply going to be a minor supplement to your income, then the cost of a package might justify the expense. It's certainly more professional and more effective than a creating one.

- Follow-up: The only real benefit commissioned salespeople can get from those sessions is a one-on-one interview with an interested attendee. So it's necessary to establish credibility, trust and interpersonal relationships. The presentations should educate but still leave unanswered questions which will be discussed privately in the post-seminar visits. The attendees should be told early on that private sessions are available.

  The forms distributed in the registration kit could be part of a system to arrange private interviews during the week or two immediately following the seminar. If the group is small enough, this can be accomplished by visiting each individual to schedule an appointment after the conclusion of the last session. If a written appointment request is used, have space for attendees to write questions or mention if there is anything in particular they want information about at your private meeting.

Seminar selling is not for everyone. More have failed than succeeded using this technique. If you decide to pursue this approach, you must give it more than just a few attempts. Successful salespeople become better presenters and more effective in organizing seminars when they establish a standard schedule and sustain it. The longer they do it, the better they become, and the more recognized they are. Word-of-mouth attendee referrals are the best source, but a loyal following takes time.

If you do pursue this approach:

- Do it right
- Do it for a significant period of time
- Pay attention to all of the issues mentioned above

ACTION PROJECT

From a Social to a Business Relationship

Being a successful salesperson presumes lots of comfortable exposure to good prospects. It also assumes the sales representative has the skill to capitalize on those opportunities and convert them to profitable sales.

Prospects can be developed from social and community activities. But sometimes target marketing is necessary. In both instances, however, top salespeople have usually developed a personal style and social skills that enhance their ability to develop a rapport that better positions them for a sale. Personality is hard to change, but the ability to perform effectively in social situations, with or without instinctive skills, can be developed. This action project addresses this skill development process. These skills will help anyone, in or out of sales, to improve their interrelationship effectiveness.

Opening the door

When two people meet for the first time, either a relationship begins or it doesn't. Two shy introverts in such a situation are likely to pass each other and nothing will happen. Two socially active and extroverted people in the same situation will greet each other and it's likely that additional conversation will follow.

Great salespeople have learned to become more outgoing and not rely on others to carry the conversation. This technique can and should be learned if it isn't instinctive.

If you find you are uncomfortable with first-time contacts, here are some techniques worth practicing which should lead to improved interrelationship skills. Check those you feel deserve your time and attention.

Situations typical of everyone's daily activities:

- *In elevators:* Enter with a happy greeting to everyone already inside; greet new arrivals.
- *At social parties:* Be sure to personally approach and introduce yourself to every person in attendance.
- *At meetings or large functions:* Scan the attendees and target not less than five people you will introduce yourself to. Use existing acquaintances to break the ice. Even if you don't know anyone, loners will appreciate your approach.
- *At stores or restaurants:* Start a conversation with the sales clerk or waiter and if possible meet the owner or manager. Also be sure to start a conversation with the cashier.
- *Other customers:* If you are forced to wait on line or in a reception area start a conversation with someone. If the other person responds then introduce yourself by name and keep the discussion going.
- *Recreational opportunities:* If it's sports, arts, hobbies or any special interest, other participants share your interest which makes starting interpersonal relationships easier and more comfortable.
- *Other situations:* The above are just illustrations of possible target opportunities. It would be a good exercise for you to add 10 specific situations you are exposed to in your daily activities. List them below (such as neighbors, commuting, doctor's/dentist's office, place of business, etc.):

1. _____

2. _____

3. _____

4. _____

5. _____

6. _____

7. _____

8. _____

9. _____

10. _____

Now practice utilizing all of these relationship opportunities.

These socially aggressive efforts will, in time, improve your social effectiveness. It will also improve your business acumen and provide additional targets for your products or services. Remember:

improved skills = improved ability to sell

What to say to extend conversation

Once the door is open, good communicators jump right in. Each of us should sharpen our conversational skills.

For many people, including me, asking pertinent questions is more effective than making a long statement. Learn to be interesting and current by staying alert to what's going on around you locally and in the world. Some of the topics below can be added to your pool of topics for conversation.

- *Current events:* Be alert to significant happenings in current news—both locally, within your state, nationally and globally.
- *Sports:* Know what teams are playing and where they stand in terms of winning and losing. This is a great jumping off point for a dialogue.
- *The instant event:* Always come prepared to address the subject being presented or discussed. Ask questions to get others talking about their interests. People love to talk.
- *Interesting stories:* Some people are effective with jokes, others are not. But everyone can prepare an interesting anecdote or two. This is a valuable part of one's repertoire.
- *Personalized approach:* If you are deliberately targeting a specific prospect, ask questions about or speak about subjects that person is likely to respond to. Sometimes pre-meeting research about the potential target is appropriate.

There are many other approaches that can be used. These examples should each be considered and extended to areas where you feel comfortable, or where another approach might be more appropriate.

Changing Social Dialogue to a Business Opportunity

If a contact leads to a comfortable interaction, it is necessary to determine whether or not the new acquaintance should be pursued as a potential sales prospect.

In chapter 9 there is a concept entitled "The Non-Interview" (I.11). It describes the technique to help position yourself for possible sales interviews. In implementing this action project, try not to conclude a first-time social dialogue with anyone until you have answered the following four questions:

Did I determine, without the target person's awareness:

Yes   No

____ ____ 1. If this person represents a potential sales prospect? Test this by the person's apparent affluence, career position, and need/use of your product or service. Are you simpatico? I don't ever pursue a relationship if I don't feel, or can't develop, a comfort level with the other person.

____ ____ 2. If this person does qualify as a potential sales prospect, when and where should I attempt to see this person again? Can I make an appointment now?

____ ____ 3. When I see this person again, which of my products or services and/or which of my sales presentations are most likely to be of interest? Which are most likely to result in a sale?

____ ____ 4. Now that I know the prospect's personality and his or her needs/wants, am I able to handle the future sales appointment alone? If not, should I bring along someone better qualified (pecking order)?

If all these questions can't be answered at the first meeting—for whatever reason—but the person appears to be a potential sales prospect because of question 1, try to arrange another visit. It can be a meal or just a cup of coffee to get to know each other better. At this more leisurely visit, try to determine the answers to 2, 3 and 4 without the new acquaintance being aware of the process.

How to Transition from a Social to a Business Relationship

It's amazing how many salespeople can't seriously discuss their products and services with people they meet away from business. I am convinced the principal reasons are the agent's basic lack of self-confidence, self-esteem, pride in their product and career, and plain old lack of enthusiasm. Those areas of weakness must be overcome.

Here is a partial checklist of methods that should be learned and utilized to make the transition from a social situation to a business one.

1. Prepare your own transition statement: First a good rapport is established. Then the potential prospect's relevant needs/wants are identified, using the non-interview technique (without the prospect's awareness). Finally, have a transitional statement you feel comfortable with so you can change the tone of the meeting from social to business.

   Here is one of mine. "John, I've really enjoyed getting to know you. I feel I've made a new friend. I look forward to seeing you often in the future. Incidentally, now that we know each other better, I feel comfortable enough to broach a subject that might be of great value to you . . ." and so on. Tailor it for your own situation. Always end with an action question such as: "Would you have time to meet with me now, or would you rather schedule a visit at a more convenient time?"

2. Assuming you can proceed, you must have an organized sales presentation that you can deliver on the spot. Seat-of-the-pants selling is for amateurs.

If you have several products and services, you probably should have multiple formal sales presentations.

Question 3 above (from the non-interview) is used to determine which sales presentation to utilize.

3. A slight attitude shift during the business portion of the conversation is appropriate. Your voice tone, body language, professionalism, should all adjust from the casual social attitude to a more competent tone, while still retaining your warm, friendly personality. This requires lots of practice. Some areas in developing your skills are:

- Professional and business-related language.
- Tight posture; a "leaning forward" style of body language.
- Competence and enthusiasm.
- Good eye contact and attentive listening.
- Relevant question-asking.
- High touch and high tech competence.

All of these skills can be utilized without ever becoming aggressive or adversarial, and while maintaining a warm personality and friendly attitude.

See chapter 9 to remind yourself what it is you are trying to achieve.

This total process, from the first-time contact with a stranger to a potential sales interview, can take 10 minutes or 10 different visits. Most great salespeople can transition on the first or second visit if they feel comfortable with a potential prospect.

Remember:
This skill area takes lots of practice.

It should be done several times every day (using both business and social opportunities).

Expect only a few of the contacts will be developed into sales prospects.

The skill developed will improve your effectiveness with all future relationships.

Great salespeople often work where they play and vice versa, which makes them 24-hour-a-day agents.

Meeting new people, whether prospects or not, is a pleasure for most sales professionals.

It is the salesperson's job to make the potential prospect comfortable, not the other way around.

8

A x S x K = $

H.1: AN OVERVIEW

To be an outstanding success, you must be able to do all parts of the job. Until you can, you will never really fully achieve your dreams and aspirations.

There are three broad areas of achievement necessary for superior salespeople:

1. Activity, which includes enough prospecting and contacting to provide a sufficient number of interviews.
2. Skill, which is the ability to get people to do what you want them to do (sometimes called selling).
3. Knowledge, appropriate to your market.

This forms the acronym ASK which looks like this:

$$A \times S \times K = \$uccess.$$

This concept works for all people since it influences others to take positive action relevant to your beliefs, products and services. For commission salespeople rate yourself in each area to predict approximately what first year commissions you will earn, using the following formula. For each factor, activity, skill and knowledge, score 0 for below an acceptable minimum performance, 1 for poor, 2 for good and 3 for excellent. This is not an exact formula, but if you then multiply your score for ASK, each point in the total (depending on your product and commission scale) should be worth a predictable amount.

I have found in complex, high-paying sales situations, each point would be worth about $15,000 in commissions per year. Hence, a poor activity level combined with poor skill and poor knowledge would generate a formula that would look like this:

A x S x K = Income *or* 1 x 1 x 1 = 1 or $15,000

Such a salesperson would generate an annual commission income of $15,000. If we could dramatically improve any one of the three talents, such as the level of activity, to the point of excellence, the formula would read:

A x S x K = I *or* 3 x 1 x 1 = 3 or $45,000

By simply improving activity, the income could jump to $45,000. No matter how well you increase activity from that point on, the income is not likely to dramatically change (unless skills and knowledge are sharpened). However, if we could get the skill up to twice the current level, moving from poor to good, the formula would now be:

A x S x K = I *or* 3 x 2 x 1 = 6 or $90,000

Income would go up to $90,000.

By concentrating on improving the weak suit, the results are most dramatic. That same salesperson could also improve knowledge from poor to good, and would now have:

$$A \times S \times K = I \ or \ 3 \times 2 \times 2 = 12 \ or \ \$180,000$$

The agent now has a potential income of $180,000. Of course, income depends on commissions and products. But the principle is the same in every business and nonbusiness situation.

Suppose a salesperson had a major failing in one or more of the ASK areas and fell below minimum. Even if the agent was excellent in skills and knowledge, but was an absolute zero in activity, the result would be:

$$A \times S \times K = I \ or \ 0 \times 3 \times 3 = 0 \ or \ failure$$

The income is below $15,000 and he or she is out of the business.

I have often heard salespeople say, "I'm a great closer, but I can't prospect." Then they proceed to fail. If that person had concentrated on prospecting at even a minimal level of activity, the formula could be:

$$A \times S \times K = 1 \ or \ 1 \times 3 \times 3 = 9 \ or \ \$135,000$$

The bottom line is: Get out of your comfort zone. Instead of bragging about your strengths, concentrate on your weak suits so your income and success level can improve. Once you have maximized your potential in one area—activity, skill or knowledge—no matter how hard you work in that comfort area, it will have little impact on your income. Giving attention to your weaker areas might be less pleasant but it can double or triple your effectiveness and income.

Eventually you will find it less unpleasant and eventually just as comfortable as your strong suits are today. It's worth doing but it's not easy. Winners are willing to pay the price.

H.2: ART VERSUS SCIENCE

One of the reasons it is so difficult to teach aspiring sales-people to sell is that there isn't one right or exclusive way to do it. But there are common denominators that can be learned. Each of us must use our natural attributes, along with the common denominators, to become the best we can. Said another way, selling is not a science but an art form.

Think about learning to dance one step at a time or painting by numbers, where a number corresponds to a particular color and you fill in the spaces.

When you are finished you can do a reasonable fox trot, but you're no Fred Astaire; or you have a picture worth framing, but by no means a masterpiece. Both dancing and art have common denominators that anyone can learn. These are actions the student takes to convert something ordinary into something unique and extraordinary. With real art, it isn't just what the artist does but how he does it. For the dancer, it's style and rhythm; for the artist, it's feeling and emotion.

Selling is clearly an art form. The basic common denominators are well established but there are many applications and interpretations. Therefore, different results are achieved. The contrast between outstanding and ordinary salespeople is not the schools they've attended or the knowledge they've acquired, but rather how they use that information to achieve their sales goals.

Said another way, it's not the words, it's the music.

Two salespeople, one successful, one marginal, can each use the same words. The end result of their efforts is solely a function of the way they sell. The raw presentation is like paint by the numbers or like the basic dance steps. It takes the addition of their enthusiasm, flair, personal power and unique skills. Sincerity and trust are an essential part of the communication process. The sales artist communicates these attributes at all times to all people.

Once you accept that selling is an art form, it becomes increasingly obvious that you don't become great just by cloning others. It's good to have role models, teachers and mentors, but don't try to precisely imitate them. Observe their techniques and their broad concepts; then take that information and interpolate it for your own style. There's no one in the world who's better at being you than yourself.

Remember, there's no right or wrong way, there's only what's right for you.

H.3: RELATIONSHIP SELLING

What's the difference between relationship (creative) selling and product selling?

Product salespeople approach every client by reviewing the relevant products they already have. Then they review their product portfolio and make new recommendations. They depend on their product's attributes to make a sale, along with their personality and the promise of service. It's just a "transaction."

Relationship (creative) salespeople begin by ignoring the products owned by their prospects and focusing on their prospects' dreams, needs and wants. They establish high-touch interpersonal relationships and sell by solving problems.

Unfortunately, there are too many product salespeople. They would be much more effective if they angled their sales toward relationships. In addition, they would offer a much greater "value added" for the prospect.

Do you want to cultivate a relationship and make sales, or do you want to just sell a product?

H.4: SALESPERSON, WHO SAYS?

When salespeople are asked what they do, I wonder how many proudly state they are salespeople.

To be a real sales pro, you must have the same discipline, knowledge and skills required of any professional, be it a doctor or a skier, golfer or tennis player. If you don't have self-discipline, if you don't study the game, if you don't practice, you will surely fail.

Why do some people in selling profess to be pros, while having a lazy work ethic, short working hours, limited knowledge and poorly honed skills? They still expect success, peer respect and financial reward even though they haven't earned it.

If sales pros hope to be successful, they must develop a routine of daily activity through disciplined prospecting and contacting. They must be organized with a work ethic that means when they work, they work, and when they play, they play. Sales efforts should consume at least 50 to 60 hours a week—more if necessary. They must have the guts to face rejection and the systems to guarantee consistency and effectiveness. They must have goals and a plan to attain them. They must be students, at least to the point of expertise for their chosen market.

Perhaps most importantly, they must be able to sell. This means taking charge of an interview and being able to get action.

Selling has become even more technical and complicated. Sadly, too many salespeople have either never learned or have forgotten how to sell. Too many trainers have become educators. It is time for those misdirected professionals to once again become salespeople.

They should, however, be even better salespeople because of more sophisticated marketing, technical support and service potential. A salesperson who can't sell, *isn't*.

H.5: OFFENSE OR DEFENSE?

Too many people are obsessed with current nonproductive problems. They spend over 80 percent of their time on minutiae and administration and less than 20 percent on productivity. The really successful achievers have reversed that ratio and are spending 80 percent of their time on productive activities and 20 percent on administration. This is possible because of systems, delegation and time control.

If we consider sales as offense, and administrative, cost control and technical concerns as defense, then it is obvious: Successful sales efforts require a maximum time commitment to offense and a minimum for defense. With aggressive selling, not administration, we can truly excel.

Our prospects are living in a very complicated and confusing era with larger and more complicated problems. Great salespeople are better positioned to address these problems than ever before. We have better products, services and technology—all at more competitive prices. Returning to our basic selling strengths will make our work more fun and more productive. We should be on the offensive between 8:00 A.M. and 6:00 P.M. with prospects, clients and centers of influence. All the defensive work (administration and paper pushing) should either be delegated to someone else or done before 8:00 A.M., after 6:00 P.M., or on weekends.

Interestingly, successful people not only spend most of their time on offense, they find it more fun than defensive work. Superior salespeople have developed the discipline of committing 80 percent of their time to offense. So can you.

H.6: QUESTIONS

Many people concerned with influencing others, whether selling or interrelating, talk too much and listen too little. To achieve our end, the less talk the better.

I have always believed that most of my prospects want to buy my product but they don't know it. Therefore, my job isn't to sell products, but to find out what the prospect wants. Until then I can't make a sale. If I want to influence friends, associates, family members or anyone, I must first find out how they feel about the subject.

You can't find out what people want by talking. You must listen. The trick, then, is to get people to talk. Hear what they say.

Of course, some talking must be done to make a sale. But not until you hear what the person is saying. To test your effectiveness, if you clocked a session you should have spent more time listening than talking before you try to sell your products or ideas.

You will know you are getting the information you need when the answers to your questions take longer than the questions. The more the prospect talks, the closer you are to a sale.

In order to get the prospect talking you have to learn to ask good questions and that is a skill in itself. In interpersonal relationships the one asking questions is on offense and the one answering is on defense. If the salesperson ends up getting backed into the corner with a machine gun blast of questions from the prospect, the seller is in trouble.

Conversely, with high-touch questions the salesperson should be getting deep insight into the feelings of the prospect so the relationship is strengthening.

To see how you rate in this skill, review your sales presentations to see who's talking more. Are the questions longer than the answers? If they are, reevaluate.

Remember, whenever you lose control of an interview, or when you seem to be losing ground in developing your ideas, turn the interview around. Buy some time for mentally regrouping by asking questions, not talking.

H.7: ARE YOU BUYING OR SELLING?

Sometimes when a salesperson returns from a sales interview, I will ask about it. The response might be that it was fantastic, but he did not make a sale. When I ask why, the answer sounds something like this:

"I did a perfect job but when I got to the close, the prospect brought out a stack of bills, showed me a checkbook with a zero balance, and, by the time we finished, I was inclined to lend him money instead of trying to sell him anything."

At other times, the same salesperson might return from an interview and respond to my inquiry with this:

"I had a fantastic interview, but even though the prospect had lots of money, he had no need for my products."

From the salesperson's perception, you might conclude that if a prospect has too little money, he cannot buy. Likewise, if he can afford it but already has what you are selling, there is no possibility of a sale.

Then who can buy? To whom do you sell?

It's a matter of which side of the coin you are inclined to look at. The salesperson can always find an excuse not to sell. You can listen to what your prospect says, and you can buy the objection rather than sell your solution. A successful salesperson would recognize that the first prospect has a fantastic need. Even though there isn't much money, the demand is overpowering and the successful salesperson would concentrate on the benefits of the product in relation to the need.

No matter how little the prospect can afford, there is little doubt that he or she could afford something, or they would not be a prospect in the first place. Your mission should be to help your prospects solve their problems, not use the problem as an excuse to avoid a solution.

Conversely, the second prospect would want to avoid

discussing what they don't have but might need. Claiming poverty, or saying they have all they need, are the ploys prospects use to discourage the average salesperson.

World-class salespeople concentrate on the prospect's goals and problems, the solution to those problems and somehow helps find the money to pay for their product.

Take two salespeople in the same situation: One would find a reason not to sell, the other might sell them both. The difference?

Attitude.

H.8: SHADES OF GRAY

After uncovering a prospect's complex and multiple problems, many salespeople find it difficult to recommend a solution. If the agent loses his self-confidence to solve the target's problem, it's likely the power to make the sale will be lost.

One approach to overcoming the salesperson's lack of confidence is to shift the decision to the prospect. Give the target three different product options and allow the client to select. While this approach can be effective, I believe it's based on weakness, not strength. I find the multiple choice approach is likely to result in indecision or, worse, the wrong decision.

In most instances the salesperson is the best qualified person to select the appropriate solution. He or she should be reasonably expert in assessing the problem and recommending the best product and/or service. Further, the buyer is almost always strongly influenced by price. So where multiple choices are provided, price rather than the "right" solution frequently determines the outcome. Many good salespeople use the multiple solution approach, so I don't suggest that you never use the smorgasbord-of-options technique.

However, I prefer picking one solution. If I can't close my first option, I have fallback alternatives that might get the prospective buyer to take some action now.

The reason some salespeople are uncomfortable making a decision is that they feel there must be only one perfect solution. It would be delightful if the world were just black and white, right or wrong, good or bad. But it isn't. There are no perfect people or perfect solutions. The real world is made up of shades of gray and none of them are absolute.

A good salesperson has the courage to diagnose the problem. Then, using his best judgment, he recommends a solution. It may not be a perfect solution. It may have some obvious flaws. But it should be the best of the available options.

To illustrate this point: I had lunch at a sales meeting with seven of the best salespeople in our entire industry. One of them asked if we would help him decide how to sell a specific prospect with a difficult problem. The one who asked the question was the most illustrious of the eight, and he explained the problem in great detail. Then each of the other seven suggested how he would handle the case. There were seven different solutions, including my own, to one specific problem.

The person who proposed the question thanked all of us and said, "I had considered each of those options." He then added one additional approach to the same problem. The point is, all eight were right. All eight would have solved the problem, but we each could only sell that which we believed was the best of the options.

Salespeople should use their knowledge and expertise to develop the best solution available. Then they must do everything in their power to help the prospect take action. If the prospect refuses, then you can turn to the next best alternate solution, even if it is a less perfect approach.

If the first recommendation doesn't solve every problem, you can still address those additional unanswered issues in the future or at the current time. Salespeople must have the courage to stand up for what they believe since it's more likely to result in the prospect taking some action.

And any action in the right direction is better than no action.

H.9: DOING THE WHOLE THING

Recently, I invited a world-class salesman to speak at one of my organization's sales meetings. He is extraordinary, earning over a million dollars a year. He has developed a reputation as a super expert in one specialized aspect of his business. Because of his unique expertise he spent most of his speech explaining his specialty and describing his current lifestyle—the result of his sales efforts. It was a great speech and all my associates had the same reaction: "Boy, that's great! I can do that!" But can they and would they pay the price?

I asked the speaker if he would mind answering a few questions. He graciously agreed. Here are a few of my queries and his answers.

Q. What time do you get up in the morning?
A. Between 4:30 A.M. and 5:00 A.M.

Q. What do you do when you get up?
A. I'm religious so I go to Mass every morning. I also work out every morning. I prepare the day and I'm in front of people by eight o'clock.

Q. How many people do you see a week?
A. I try to see three to five people a day, every day, but no less than 15 a week. [In his business, that's a full workload.]

Q. How many sales do you make a year?
A. Several hundred. [Again, in his industry most salespeople have trouble maintaining one sale a week.]

Another outstanding salesman once described an interesting and unusual work system. He said that he did all of his phone contacting two days a week—Monday and Wednesday—and didn't stop working the telephone until he had filled up Tuesday and Thursday with appointments in a "client" firm, scheduled every half hour. On selling days a good salesperson in our business might see three to five people per day. He was seeing as many as 15.

He explained that sometimes an interview took longer than 30 minutes. In those cases he'd cancel and reschedule the next appointment, sticking with the first one until the sale was consummated. That was his Monday through Thursday schedule. It gave him Friday off. He was an extraordinarily disciplined and very effective salesperson. What the audience heard, and emulated, was you can work four days and take Friday off.

Since I had initially hired and trained him, I knew that in his early days he was a 6½-day-a-week person. He was in the office every weekend, and the other five days of the week he worked in the field selling.

If you are going to emulate great successes, it's necessary to learn what the great ones did to get there. Then you have to adjust your routine accordingly and pay the necessary price. Eventually, you will become a unique individual.

Remember: You can't build a career doing only the things you enjoy. You've got to do the whole thing.

H.10: GREATER PRODUCTIVITY

In order to succeed in an inflationary environment, sales-people must constantly increase their income just to maintain their living standards.

Either increasing the number of sales or making larger sales are the two ways to boost a commission salesperson's income. Only by doing both concurrently can salespeople be relatively sure of not just holding their own but of constantly growing. Fortunately, such a program is attainable if you are adaptable.

Almost all sales professionals now have portfolios with a large variety of products in different price categories, some with bells and whistles, some without. There should also be a diversity of products that perform different functions. Almost all qualified prospects or existing clients buy something in the salesperson's portfolio at regular intervals.

Since technology is increasing so rapidly, clients and prospects have ever-increasing needs. Obsolescence is happening at an astronomical pace. Also, the typical prospect today is working with larger cash flows than ever before.

Therefore, despite higher expenses and lower per-unit commissions, the opportunities have never been better for the sales professional.

If salespeople previously sold one in three closing attempts (which is not an unusual ratio), they should be able to sell at least one in every two attempts. Commissions should be higher because of multiple or large-quantity sales and higher-priced products.

The compound growth results from seeing more people, selling to a higher percentage of those seen, and making larger average sales. Of course, if activity goes down and the improved sales skill doesn't increase, the salesperson is in trouble. The good news: The decision for success or failure will be determined solely by the salesperson and his or her capacity to adapt to the marketing environments and the products and services available to address them.

The opportunities are tremendous.

H.11: PICK UP YOUR CHANGE

It is surprising how little time is spent teaching salespeople to work more intelligently and how much effort is spent trying to make them work harder.

It's true that most salespeople must develop the habit of starting earlier, working later and seeing more clients. But much could be accomplished by getting them to achieve more from the efforts they are already expending. Here are some "work smarter, not harder" ideas:

- *Additional Sale:* Often a prospect would buy more on the sales interview if given the opportunity. When you know there are other products or services needed, and that they are affordable, don't stop selling after the first sale. And always ask for referrals.

- *Other Sales:* Even if the prospect rejects the primary sale, automatically start another using a completely different product or approach. Also consider if there are other potential targets in the original prospect's business or family situation.

- *Chain Sales:* After a successful sales effort, either right then, or on product delivery, begin a new sales presentation from a completely new perspective. Don't let the chain break until the client says no.

- *Make the Sale Larger:* If the target has bought a product make sure you show an additional one of either bigger volume or one that does a great deal more for a relatively small additional cost. (In some product situations this might be done more effectively at the product delivery.)

9

Positioning for the Sale

I.1: AN OVERVIEW

A one-for-one closing ratio seems impossible to most sales-people. Yet some great salespeople claim they are capable of closing every sale.

World-class salespeople have learned to work through a process that precedes any attempt to actually close a sale. If that process is not completed to the salesperson's satisfaction, no attempt to sell is initiated. The sales process is either aborted or postponed. I know by instinct when it's time to make the sale. At that point I can close almost everyone so, in effect, I am closing every sale I attempt to close.

Learning to position yourself, cultivating interrelationships, and using high-touch skills, should precede every sales effort. In this section we will explore those skills and procedures.

I.2: PROBLEM SOLVING

Solving problems, not product selling, is the key to success. Regardless of the quality of the product, it is likely that someone else has something cheaper. Salespeople who are trying to sell, based solely on the product, are likely to find competition costing them a great many sales. On the other hand, taking the time and trouble to find out what is disturbing the prospect, and then recommending appropriate solutions to his or her problem, can change a lost sale into a successful effort.

The client is really buying the representative's skill, knowledge and service—not necessarily a specific product. Of course, the price of the product must be justified by the product's true value. However, it doesn't have to be the cheapest. Successful salespeople will sell products that may not be the least expensive, but will still be a bargain. You get what you pay for.

The most successful salespeople start the process with an open mind. They elicit information from the prospect that will help identify the problems, needs and wants. Then they design a plan to solve the problem. The classic analogy is that though many people buy drills in hardware stores, the public does not want drills, it wants holes.

I work with several attorneys and their rates run from as little as $25 an hour to as high as $200 an hour. If the service and benefits justify the cost, $200 an hour is a good deal. But if they fail to fulfill my requirements, $25 an hour is certainly no bargain.

1.3: LISTENING

The key to successful selling and interpersonal relationships is not necessarily a result of talking but a direct result of listening. This is discussed in chapter 8 (H.6).

But what is listening?

Hearing what comes through your ears is part of the answer—but a surprisingly small part. Some people will outright lie but most will lie by omission. Unless they already trust and respect you, there are many things people will avoid talking about. Most people in an impersonal situation will tell you what they think you want to hear—or simply not say anything.

If you can't get prospects to open up, they probably will not "buy" you or your products, ideas or services. You will be further disadvantaged because they won't tell you why they really do or don't agree with your position.

So what is listening?

It's not hearing. It's learning what the other person thinks and feels. To do that effectively you must use your ears, eyes and sometimes touch.

Eye contact is very important, as is body language. They can tell you as much as words. Is the person comfortable? Is he telling the truth? Is there something left out?

It's also a two-way street. Are your eyes darting all over the place? Do you really care? Are you concentrating? Is there a comfortable relationship between the two of you?

When you ask a question, is the answer significantly longer than the question, or the other way around?

A competent interviewer can ask a question that not only gets an answer, but also gets additional relevant thoughts that go beyond the scope of the original question.

Listening is an art.

If you can get a person talking, you have a better chance of figuring out what he is really saying. Great influencers learn to think like the prospect.

To be a success at this ask yourself:

- Is the person concerned about the current issue?
- Is he being truthful?
- Why does the person feel that way?
- Does he really trust me?

The bottom line is that all aspiring successes must learn to get the prospect talking freely and with trust. You must learn when their observations are relevant and when to keep your mouth shut and listen. In the early part of interviews, you must use questions to get the other person talking. Once the communication begins, it's time to sit back and listen until you really have learned enough to state your position effectively.

I.4: FIVE PARTS OF THE SALE

The sales procedure (see I.10) is a skill function which must be learned and personalized to fit the style and personality of the salesperson.

It might include a standard structured presentation, or it might be a basic process that has proven effective.

Since the procedure reflects the sales representative, the product being sold, the problem it addresses and the prospect being sold, there are as many procedures as there are sellers. So the end result boils down to the salesperson's skill.

The sales procedure embraces five distinct parts which I have defined as the "Anatomy of the Sale."

The simpler the sale (such as a clerk in a department store), the more you can take liberties with the five parts and still achieve success. The truly great salespeople, in the most difficult selling positions, include all five parts in every presentation.

Of course, the worst salesperson will occasionally sell something and the best still won't sell everybody. But by doing it right, and carefully touching every one of the five steps, the success ratio will greatly improve.

The five parts which make up the skeleton of a super presentation are described in detail on the following pages. They are:

- Selling yourself (being simpatico)
- Selling your expertise/service (being competent)
- Finding the want/need (identifying the problem)
- Selling the benefit (finding a solution)
- Selling the product (closing the deal)

Your sales presentation should include all five parts. When you critique an unsuccessful sales effort, be objective. Don't just blame your close, but review your effectiveness in each of the five areas.

I.5: SELLING YOURSELF

Typical salespeople remember every client, but quickly forget the ones they failed to sell. Why does this happen? Is it because you remember those you sell or sell those you will remember?

We see so many people they become indistinguishable blurs. I have seen a salesperson walk right by someone he made a presentation to just days before with no recognition. When there is not a real personal-touch relationship, people don't remember.

An extreme example of this happened when I joined a salesperson on a second interview with a prospect seen one week earlier. After the initial greeting, some small talk and several minutes of the sales interview, the prospect interrupted and said, "I remember you. You're the fellow that was here last week and asked me all those questions."

We had been in the presence of the prospect for over five minutes before he even remembered who the salesperson was—even though he spent an hour with him one week before.

Often we leave no personal impression on a prospect nor do they on us. Usually, those would not have led to a successful sale anyway. People buy from (and share their personal and/or business lives with) people they trust and respect. Yet, most of the time, salespeople skip that part of the presentation and get right down to business—without first selling themselves.

The textbooks on selling suggest that we find some common interest or dress in an appealing manner. Though I do not deny the validity of these and other approaches, they are not enough unto themselves.

The best way to sell yourself is to say as little as possible. Get the prospect to talk, then listen.

At a social function, are you impressed or turned off by an individual who dominates the conversation? Most people are bored with domineering people. Conversely, if you have a good dialogue with someone, and they show a serious interest in you, don't you leave feeling he was a really nice person?

If salespeople began every first interview with leading questions, allowed the prospect to share special interests and really listened, they would accomplish two things:

1. They would sell themselves.
2. They would get valuable information which might help later in the sales process.

I.6: SELLING YOUR EXPERTISE

Having sold yourself, you must now sell your expertise. This is another area where most marginal agents lose ground. Even the better producers often miss the boat.

A classic complaint that I often hear from weak salespeople is: "I won't sell prospect A because I don't want to impose on my friends and relatives, and I can't sell prospect B because he has a relative in the business."

Superior salespeople, however, sell their own friends and relatives, as well as the competing salesperson's friends and relatives!

I have close friends who are lawyers, accountants, physicians and dentists. But I chose my lawyer, accountant, physician and dentist on a combination of a reasonably good interpersonal relationship and, more importantly, on their expertise.

It is no surprise therefore that many of my clients have friends and relatives who sell the same products I sell, but they choose to buy from me. That is not because they like me better but because they think I am more qualified and they want the best they can get.

Unlike selling yourself, the sale of your competence requires self-confidence, education and enthusiasm. We must communicate success and expertise, but we must also earn the credentials that stand the test of time.

I.7: FINDING THE NEED

Before you can sell any product to a prospect, the prospect must recognize that a problem or need exists. Assuming that you know what the prospect needs or wants is often the salesperson's downfall. Be careful when you assume that every married person loves his spouse or wants to send the kids to college. Not everyone puts their family's well-being ahead of their own comfort.

Beware when you presume every business wants to be on the cutting edge. Everyone doesn't want a new car or a large-screen TV. Every person you meet doesn't necessarily want or need your product or service.

Find out what the prospect's dreams are in relation to your product or service before attempting to sell anything. The prospect's right to have personal preferences is a fact of life. Resist the temptation to transfer your own values, ethics, morals and desires to the prospect.

Can you imagine a car salesman who loves Corvettes selling one to a man with six children who is in the market for a family car?

Listen with an open mind to determine the prospect's real dreams and aspirations (needs/wants). In the above example, the car salesperson could easily learn that this particular prospect wants transportation for a family of eight. The solution, of course, would be a van. Now a sale is possible.

The car analogy makes the point that super salespeople don't try to sell anything until they take the time, with a completely open mind, to learn what the prospect wants. Then, if a product in the salesperson's portfolio will solve the prospect's problem, a sales effort should be initiated. (Which means that if there were no vans in the dealer's inventory, the agent would still not try to sell a Corvette but might try a station wagon instead.)

I.8: SELLING THE BENEFIT

Instinctively, the typical agent believes that the solution to every problem must be a product he sells. Nothing could be further from the truth. Typical prospects do not care a bit about my product, per se. What they want to know is if the purchase they make will solve *their* problems and satisfy *their* needs. The salesperson must couch the solution in terms of benefits, not features.

It is not uncommon for a life insurance agent to say, "Mr. Prospect, the solution to your problem is an ordinary life policy with a term rider attached. We can add a guaranteed insurability rider, plus disability waiver of premium and additional indemnity."

Although the insurance agent fully understands what he just said, it doesn't mean a thing to the prospect. The agent has expressed the solution in terms of the features of the product. Most prospects won't understand how these features will solve their problems.

It would be better to say, "Mr. Prospect, the solution I recommend will provide an income for your wife and children, will keep them in their own world; will accumulate cash for yourself as a future source of capital like a savings account; and will cost you very little in comparison to the security it will provide. If you are disabled, you won't have to continue the payments—they will be paid for you. And, if you should die as a result of an accident, I have arranged for substantial additional benefits for your wife and children."

Both statements fairly accurately describe the recommended solution. The first one concerns itself with the product (the features); the second addresses the needs of the prospect (the benefits).

Since the benefits are what the client identifies with, that is what the salesperson must sell. This is where the expression

"Sell the sizzle, not the steak" came from. Unfortunately, the instinct of most salespeople is to sell the steak (product), whereas the prospect will only buy the sizzle (benefit).

Regardless of the idea, product or service you are trying to sell, be sure to spend significant time on the benefits to the prospect and only as much time as is absolutely necessary on the technical features. For example, if it is appropriate, particularly emphasize cost savings, efficiency, tax savings, reduction in number of employees or speed, and accentuate the relationship to the prospect's wants as established in the preceding concepts.

I.9: SELLING THE PRODUCT

By this point in the interview you have done an effective job selling yourself, selling your expertise and your service, establishing the needs/wants of the prospect and presenting a benefit or solution using language the prospect can understand. Up until this point, master salespeople have omitted any reference to a specific product or the cost and have exclusively addressed the wants of the prospect. If this has been done effectively, all that remains is selling the product.

You know what the prospect wants. There is good rapport between you and the prospect. You have established your professional credibility. And you have agreed that there is an acceptable solution to the problem.

The closing process begins by presuming that the prospect has bought the solution and is now ready to buy your product. On occasion that's all that's necessary. Filling out an order form will complete the sale. However, there is often delay, indecision and questions that must be addressed. At this point the features of your product must be effectively presented while using your closing skills.

The key here is to help the prospect take action without developing a combative, adversarial or aggressive posture.

The five parts of a sale are the structural components that are the science of selling. In actual practice the art of the sale is done by developing a procedure to accomplish these ends.

I.10: THE PROCEDURE

We've just described the scientific anatomy of the sale. I've broken the process down into five smaller sales which should all be included in every interview to achieve maximum sales effectiveness.

But remember, selling is not a science, it is an art form. The five parts of the sale help construct the words that should be verbalized; the key to achieving excellence is the music of selling. That is the procedure or the art form.

It is important for artists to learn the basic fundamentals so they can apply their unique skills and produce a finished work of art. Likewise for the salesperson. The five parts outlined above and incorporated into every interview, will be enhanced by the magic (or skill) of the salesperson and the deal can be closed.

The actual script used for the anatomy of the sale can be any sales presentation that the salesperson or company feels appropriate. An organized sales track is certainly a good start for most salespeople, and it usually includes the fundamentals the salesperson/artist must learn.

The difference is the magic that transforms an ordinary sales presentation into an extraordinary one. The process described as follows should be superimposed on the organized sales presentation. If done correctly it will enhance the basic premise by adding the unique personality and power of the salesperson.

The following five concepts deal with the artistic side of the selling process.

1. Uncover the prospect's goals, dreams and aspirations (needs/wants).

2. Find out what the prospect has already done to achieve those wants.

3. If what has been done is inadequate to solve the problem, take away the prospect's dream.

4. Then return the dream by offering a creative solution.

5. Close the sale.

I.11: THE NON-INTERVIEW

The non-interview is a technique that is exactly what the name implies—a visit that does not look or feel like a formal interview. Such an approach may seem self-evident, but many people have difficulty achieving it. It's not unusual for a salesperson to literally change his natural voice, posture and language when the selling hat is on. I have observed people in a comfortable, normal social situation appear relaxed. I've then seen those same people in a new and uncomfortable social situation or in direct contact with a potential prospect appear nervous and tense. It's hard to believe they are the same individuals.

The language becomes formal and stiff, the smile is gone, the voice is serious and deeper (or higher and squeakier if nerves are on edge). There is no apparent warmth for the person being addressed and the individual appears to be thinking of what to say next, instead of listening to what is being said.

This altered personality is totally counterproductive from both a social and sales point of view. Such behavior can lose deals because the prospect never gets to see the real you. Most sales are at least partially influenced by the interpersonal relationship established before the business interview begins. Successful people have developed the skill to be even friendlier and warmer on an interview than in their personal life, rather than the other way around. The non-interview technique, when mastered, will help you achieve that skill.

The first time you meet someone new (whether it's at a social function, supermarket, on a cold canvass visit or at a scheduled appointment) begin with what I have dubbed the non-interview.

To help explain this approach, think about having a social dinner at a friend's house. Before the evening is over you will have a comfortable rapport with one or more of the other guests. If you meet again there will be immediate recognition and a friend-liness. On the other hand, there may have been other people at that dinner you might not remember the next day.

Commission salespeople can charm a great diversity of per-sonalities. They are truly masters of the non-interview. To learn this process, you must first become aware of the changes in your voice pattern, personality and language in stressful situa-tions. When you first meet people learn to initiate nonthreaten-ing conversation with friendly attitudes, accompanied by consistent body language and charisma.

Actually, the non-interview technique can be used to accom-plish the first two parts of the five parts of the sale: selling your-self and selling your expertise. However, the non-interview has no business implications. It lasts as long as it takes to complete those two parts of the sale, and is accomplished without the other person being aware of the process. Often the non-interview will also begin the third part of the sale, uncovering what the potential prospect wants to achieve in areas relevant to your products and services.

I will not attempt a formal sales presentation unless I suc-cessfully complete the non-interview. The non-interview can be done in minutes or may take many visits. It can be done play-ing 18 holes of golf or during a social evening with new acquaintances. For people you see periodically, but rarely have private time with, it can be done over a long period of time with many brief, superficial contacts.

With each passing contact and with high touch, the relation-ship can be strengthened. Typical of these multiple brief non-interviews are neighbors, fellow members in organizations, fellow commuters.

When I make a sales appointment with someone I have never met, perhaps a referred lead, I begin the actual interview with the non-interview. If I never develop a comfortable interrelationship

I don't try to make the sale. The non-interview is the first step of positioning because it encourages the potential prospect to share his dreams and aspirations and it helps get answers to questions that help determine what to do next.

Four questions that help prepare for a subsequent sales effort and that you should attempt to answer for yourself during the non-interview are:

Q. Is this a person I wish to proceed with?
A. If you are not comfortable with the person or they're not simpatico with you, or if the person doesn't qualify as someone in your desired target market, or if the person does not seem interested in your products and services, there is no reason to proceed.

Q. If I decide to proceed, when should I do it?
A. Even if the non-interview was the beginning of what was intended to be a sales presentation, or if the contact was at a social event, it may not be appropriate to proceed with a business-related interview at that particular time. Of course, if the circumstances are correct, you may proceed with the sales interview, but in all other situations it is better to arrange another appointment at a more suitable time and place.

Q. Which idea, product or service is most likely to be appropriate for this person?
A. With an in-depth non-interview you know the special interests, needs and wants of the prospect. Thus, you increase your probability of making a sale. Presuming you have multiple products and/or sales presentations, the non-interview helps determine which of the presentations in your inventory are most likely to result in a sale.

Q. Am I qualified to handle this situation by myself?

A. Sometimes the non-interview makes the salesperson aware that the complexity of the problem, the personality of the prospect or the products required to solve the problem are beyond his capacity or comfort level. If there is a potential for a very large sale, it may be appropriate to bring a more mature expert along on the sales interview, even if it means a split commission. Fifty percent of something is better than 100 percent of nothing. The salesperson's initial instincts about his ability to handle the prospect are usually correct.

I.12: THE PROSPECT'S WANTS, GOALS, DREAMS

Qualified prospects have wants which are probably relevant to your ideas, products and services. Unfortunately, potential prospects may not be aware of it. Even if they are, they may not share it with you. In fact, if the interview is formal, stressful or adversarial the prospect will not open up at all. However, if you begin every sales interview with a low profile, non-interview antagonism can be avoided.

Instead, you can develop a warm relationship that creates a mutually comfortable feeling. Then, if you listen and not talk, it is probable these wants will be shared—along with problems and frustrations.

Since the non-interview is conducted without a pad or any other business materials, the effective communicator listens and records in the back of his or her mind an impression of what the prospect wants to accomplish and why it has not already been done.

- Be relaxed.
- Listen with your eyes.
- Watch for body language signals.
- Communicate with interest, concern and compatibility.

If you can get the prospect to share his dreams and goals, you are on the way to a potentially successful relationship.

During this same low profile, nonadversarial, non-interview, it's appropriate for the salesperson to share his dreams and aspirations—including his business and personal life. Remember, to make a prospect into a customer then into a client, you must open up, too.

Strong personal relationships begin at the initial greeting. To help get the prospect talking, organize your questions into four different categories. Some of the sought-after information is absolutely irrelevant to making a sale but it does help sell the salesperson to the prospect. And it can develop a high-touch relationship. The four categories are:

1. *Family situation.* Questions about marital status, children, home, future plans, etc.

2. *Personal.* Questions relevant to retirement plans, special interests and hobbies, lifestyle expectations, wealth accumulation, etc.

3. *Business.* Questions about the success of their business (if they have a business), size of business, how it started, where it might be going, when they might want to sell or retire, who might take it over, and of course specialty questions directly relevant to your products and services.

4. *Special interests and charities.* Questions about extracurricular activities, organizations, sports or cultural interests, favorite charities, political involvements, community activities.

Don't ask all of the questions all the time. Just get the conversation started, then keep it going until you feel comfortable with the prospect. If the prospect also feels at ease with you, some of his dreams, wants and aspirations will be revealed. Since the prospect knows what you are selling, it's likely that the topics discussed will in part relate to those products and services.

This part of the interview can take as little as five minutes if the target already knows you or if you are simpatico.

It also can take many hours. One of the largest sales I ever made was to a delightful family who operated an immense ranch in California. I had been referred by close mutual friends. The ranch was a three-hour trip each way and I was anxious to get to business and get back home. When I began the sales process I moved much too quickly from the non-interview to an attempt to sell. After I asked some pointed and personal questions, the older rancher stopped me and said, "Who do you think you are coming here from the big city and treating us like we're country bumpkins?"

It was like a splash of cold water. He was right, I was wrong. I had broken my own cardinal rule.

I immediately apologized and said this wasn't my normal style. I knew something about him so I thought I understood his problem. Since I faced a long drive back, I pushed too fast.

He said, "That might be the case but you still had no right asking me those personal questions."

I agreed and suggested the following: "I promise I won't ask any more questions nor attempt to sell you anything today. I apologize for having been too aggressive, that's not my normal style. However, since I'm here, I'd like the opportunity to get to know you. How about if I stopped selling and just listened?"

Without much enthusiasm he said okay, but I was starting out in big trouble.

We spent the balance of the morning doing a non-interview. As I listened, he saw my sincere interest and when lunchtime arrived he invited me to stay. Then he showed me around the ranch. During all this time I never even hinted about my business.

Finally, late in the day, I suggested it was probably time for me to start back to San Francisco. By then I felt like I had made a new friend and apparently he felt the same way. As I was about to leave I said, "I won't come back unless you invite me, but let me send you some material about my organization and the kind of work I do. I'll give you references from people I think you'd respect. I'll call you in a few weeks but I'd rather have you as a friend than as an unhappy prospect. Is that okay?" He agreed and we shook hands and I left.

The next day I sent him a substantial package of materials and contacted some mutual friends and asked them to call or write him. Two weeks later I called. It was like talking to a friend. He offered to send one of his planes to fly me back and forth. On the very next interview I made the largest sale of my career (at that point in time).

As I've said, the non-interview can take five minutes or all day. It's a judgment call based on the possible size of the sale, the level of your personal relationship and how much time you want to invest in the process. This part of the relationship can't be a memorized track. To be good at the non-interview you must develop communication skills that are uniquely you. No two interviews will ever be exactly alike.

This concept concerns the use of the non-interview to get the prospect to voluntarily share his thoughts. The sale I made to my rancher friend would have been impossible on the second interview—which was really the first selling interview—had I not heard the wants and problems on my first visit. Selling is easy when you find out what the prospect needs and how your products or services can solve the problem.

Try these possible openings:

- I'm very pleased to meet you, but I don't know you nearly as well as I would like. Regardless of whether or not we ever do business, I'd enjoy getting to know you better. Would you mind chatting with me for a few minutes?

- I know there are certain important matters we intend to discuss. But like a physician, I feel uncomfortable recommending solutions to a problem before we get to know each other better and I learn more about your concerns. Would you mind if I ask you a few questions before we get to the business part of our meeting?

Any approach along that line gets it going, but I'm often asked, "How do you get that dialogue to be as effective as possible in positioning yourself to make a sale?"

Although many prospects initially appear negative about buying anything, there are always important things they want to achieve, for themselves, their business or their loved ones. These are strong emotional priorities. The trick is to find out what the prospect really wants, not needs, in a nonthreatening way. The specific questions depend on each situation but I address the four categories listed at the start of this concept.

I will not proceed with a sales presentation if I have not developed a strong understanding of the prospect and have not established a comfortable relationship. The more relaxed and the less structured this part of the interview process is, and the more sincere, caring, sharing and empathetic you are, the more likely you are to get meaningful information. Besides the areas already suggested, you should develop a series of questions particularly relevant to your products and services in order to specifically get want/goal/need information for the prospect's unique situation.

If done effectively, this positioning prior to the sales interview will significantly increase the sales probability.

I.13: WHAT HAVE THEY DONE
ABOUT THEIR DREAMS?

To effectively continue the sales process, you must be able to identify the dreams, expectations and goals of the prospect as they relate to your product or service. So far there should have been no discussion of what you are selling and no arguments or competitive challenges. Grow comfortable with each other.

Since most of your relationship so far has been as a non-interview, you now must switch to a business relationship. A good transitional statement helps move the interview to the next phase. The transitional statement can be as simple as: "Gosh, we've been talking for 30 minutes and we've never discussed the real reason we've gotten together in the first place. Though I'm not positive my products are the solution to your problems, I suspect they are. Like a doctor, I don't prescribe a product (or service) until I examine the patient. Would you mind answering some questions so that I can find out if, and how, my products (services) can help you achieve your personal objectives?"

This concept can be communicated in many different ways, as long as it is accomplished. Then, if you're using an organized sales track, you proceed with the data-gathering or fact-finding process. This is the first time you take out any materials and begin what appears to be a formal interview.

The prospect's perception is that the interview is just beginning, when, in fact, the interview actually began when you first said hello. What you learned during the non-interview has given you a pretty good idea as to the personality, current situation and the objectives of the prospect. What you don't yet know is what he has done to achieve the objectives and how the situation relates to your products and services. The facts you get will answer these questions.

I rarely find a need/want during data gathering that I didn't already uncover in the non-interview. However, once you determine the current situation and compare it to the objectives, you will know whether or not the prospect has an unresolved problem that you can solve. Even when you uncover some significant unfulfilled need, you maintain your professional manner and control your emotions. Avoid confrontation; don't interrupt the process to attempt a sale. Prospects may ask questions that can distract you from the sales process. Respond with, "We'll get to that, now let's continue."

One reason for not allowing yourself to get distracted is that even if an obvious sales opportunity presents itself, there may be a more critical one not yet uncovered. Also, there may be problems or objectives not yet identified.

Stay on track until you learn all you can learn about the present situation. You don't want to discuss product or cost. Don't allow any possibility of a disagreement until you are completely positioned for the sale. If the first part of the process was done effectively, this second step will establish whether or not a gap exists between what the prospect is attempting to achieve, and what has been done about getting there.

Most importantly, there is a nonadversarial, warm and friendly, interpersonal relationship developing which allows you to move to the third step which follows.

I.14: TAKE IT AWAY

When steps one (goals, wants and dreams) and two (what have they done about them) are completed, and it's obvious that what the prospect has will not achieve what he wants, it is necessary to disturb the prospect so that he shares your concern about the inadequacy of the present situation.

The best way to get the prospect emotionally disturbed is to review the information that has been shared. Then say that based on the current situation, the dream or want is not likely to be fulfilled.

Telling the prospect there's a problem won't get the job done. The prospect must accept and understand the problem and be sincerely concerned and disturbed. For example, if the prospect wants to significantly expand the size of the business, and the current equipment couldn't hold up under the pressure of the large additional volume of work, the salesperson should congratulate the prospect on the ambition. But point out it can't happen without changing the business machines.

Some prospects are aware they have a serious problem and you get immediate agreement. On other occasions prospects may try to defend or rationalize their position to prove that they really don't have a problem at all. With the first group you're ready to move on to step four. However, for the group that is denying the existence of a problem, it is necessary to spend additional time to get agreement and concern.

Review their wants and objectives to make sure you understood what they are trying to accomplish. If you get reinforcement of their objectives, you must review their current status to make sure there really is a gap between what they have now and what they are trying to achieve. If that is confirmed, show that the way they're currently positioned, their goals are not likely to be achieved. If there is still resistance it's time to listen

and find out why the prospect doesn't think they have a problem. Then try and get concurrence by asking questions. The
more they talk (presuming your analysis of the situation is correct) the more likely they are to eventually say: "I've never
thought about it quite that way but I guess you're right. I do
have a problem."

There's no need to change your regular sales presentation as
the skeleton for your selling efforts, but achieving each step in
the sales procedure is the key to success.

Here is a sports-related analogy to make the point. There are
many golfers that look good and appear to swing the club correctly, but can't hit the ball cleanly or in the right direction. Their
balance, rhythm and tempo are wrong.

Think of your sales presentation as your balance and consider
the procedure as the timing and tempo. Is your timing and personal involvement with high-touch relationships part of the
sales interview?

Are you sure you don't move from one part of the presentation
to the next before you've completed each part of the procedure?

We have determined wants, found out what they've got, and
then disturbed them by taking away what they want because of
how they're currently positioned. Once you achieve that level of
disturbance, you're very close to being fully positioned to make
the sale.

I.15: GIVE IT BACK

The prospect acknowledges there is a serious problem.

You are aware of the wants.

You know what the prospect has done about the problem.

You have disturbed the prospect by taking away the want.

Now you are close to beginning the real closing sales process.

In the past three parts of the procedure, we have simply been positioning ourselves for making the sale. There's been no confrontation, no attempt to argue about preconceived notions, no discussion of product, cost or features. We are simply examining the patient, so to speak. Agent and prospect both understand the problem and both are disturbed.

The next step is to reduce the stress level. That's why you are there.

One of the greatest salespeople of all time explained this concept by saying, "Mr. Prospect, you have a problem but don't worry about it. When I walk out that door I'll take your problem with me and you're going to be fine."

If the prospect seems positive about resolving the problem you can proceed with what I call the "benefit statement." This technique requires that you restate the problem as you perceive it, using the same words that the prospect used to explain his or her concerns.

The structure follows this pattern: "Mr. Prospect, as I understand it, you want to achieve certain goals which we have identified [in the real interview you would restate those goals] and I think you agree the way you are currently positioned those goals will not be achieved. Now if I could show you a way to accomplish precisely what it is you want to do, at a cost that you could afford, am I correct in assuming that you would be interested in implementing such a plan?"

Obviously, you would phrase that statement to suit the circumstance and to reflect your own personality. If you can get an agreement to that type of statement you have completed the first four parts of the sales process and you are finally fully positioned to make the sale.

What you should have so far is:

- A good interpersonal relationship.
- A mutual respect based on trust and perceived expertise.
- An awareness of the prospect's attitude relevant to his or her wants, relating to your product areas and the problems influencing the current situation.
- A mutual concern about the problem.
- A mutual desire to try and solve the problem.

And most importantly, up until now there have been no confrontations, adversarial stress, or arguments between you and the prospect. You both have traveled a path of mutual interest and benefit.

I.16: MAKING THE SALE

This is the last step in the selling process. The seller has performed effectively. A good relationship has been established. The facts have been documented. The existence of a problem has been agreed upon. And the seller has the assurance that if a solution can be developed the prospect will give it serious consideration.

You are ready to complete the sale.

To illustrate positioning, let me share a story. A super salesman who had often stated that he had nearly a one-for-one closing ratio had a son who followed in his footsteps. Like most new salespeople, the son had a difficult time early in his career. After months of frustration he finally turned to his dad and asked, "Would you mind spending a day in the field with me and giving me some pointers?"

The father agreed, and they spent an entire day together. The son had scheduled a day full of back-to-back interviews; mostly with people he didn't previously know whom he had not pre-qualified. Nonetheless, they were optimistic and enthusiastic about the prospects that lay ahead. When the day was over, they had struck out every time. Not one sale had been made.

On the way home the son said, "Dad, whatever happened to that one-for-one baloney you talk about?"

The question awakened the father to the great value of positioning. He realized in retrospect that, in his own career, he selected qualified prospects and spent adequate time properly positioning for the sale. This kept his closing percentage almost perfect. If he wasn't positioned correctly, he didn't attempt the close.

The super-salesman father then explained to the son that he had to prepare the prospect (with the positioning process) prior to trying to sell, if he wanted to close most of his attempts. The son learned quickly and is now a budding star in his own right.

That incident reinforces the basic concept of the sales process and positioning. If the salesperson is properly positioned, the sale itself is relatively easy. However, positioning doesn't ensure a sale. The typical prospect doesn't usually demand to buy something. Most products still have to be sold. But to attempt to sell without positioning can result in a day with many interviews and not a single sale.

The final part of the sales process is to make the sale by getting action, sometimes called closing.

In addition to everything mentioned in this chapter, the salesperson must have the right mental attitude. There must be a conviction that the solution being offered is the correct one for the problem. There must be enthusiasm and power to communicate with confidence. The agent's attitude must imply that the prospect's best choice is to accept the recommendation—that the cost of not taking action will be greater than the cost of taking action. In other words, the salesperson has to approach the close with complete conviction and the power to influence action.

I.17: HOW MANY SALES INTERVIEWS FOR ONE SALE?

Many salespeople have products and services that are classically sold in one interview. More complicated sales situations may require several visits. In some instances, particularly in the more complex technological areas, multiple visits are the rule. The question is: How many interviews are right for you?

I have already described the anatomy of the sale, which identifies the five parts of the sales structure, and I also described the sales procedure which also has five parts. Does this mean there should be five interviews?

Absolutely not.

The skill of the salesperson, the products and services he has in his portfolio, the complexity of the prospect's problems, and the decision-making time required by the prospect determine the number of interviews necessary. There could be as few as one—or as many as necessary. Naturally, the fewer the interviews to complete one sale, the more effective the productivity and profitability of the salesperson will be.

In practice this means the five parts can be done in one interview or they can be broken up into several interviews, but there are some basic rules to help maximize your effectiveness.

- Never begin a benefit statement and/or a close unless you have all the ammunition you need to complete the transaction. If it can't be done during that particular interview, then schedule a subsequent interview for the benefit statement and the close.

- Once you begin to share specifics about your products and/or your proposed solution to the prospect's problem and you don't complete the sale, you have lost your best chance to make a sale.

- The moment an unsuccessful closing interview is concluded, the typical prospect will discuss your solution and products with other people, all of whom suddenly become experts. Often they will comparison shop which means the salesperson will be in a weaker position on the next interview.

- However, if the interview is aborted once the prospect's problems are identified, and the prospect is disturbed about the present situation, and the salesperson promises to be back with a solution, the next interview—which might well be the closing interview—begins with a sense of urgency and interest on the part of the prospect. They always are curious about seeing your solution to their problem whether they expect to buy or not.

- If you can't be sure you can conclude a sale in one interview, abort and schedule a second.

- If it takes longer to cultivate a good relationship with a particular prospect, this can also result in an additional interview.

Other reasons for additional interviews might include: (1) a key decision-maker's absence; (2) not enough information from the prospect to design a recommended solution; (3) not being fully positioned to complete the sale; (4) running out of either the prospect's or the agent's time; (5) outside distractions which lead to rescheduling to another time and place; (6) the need to do more research on potential products for a solution to the prospect's problems.

Though the fewer interviews it takes to make one sale will contribute to the salesperson's efficiency, rushing a sale will often end with no sale. The instincts and skills one develops will determine how many interviews are right for that particular prospect. The salesperson would be well advised to be crisp and efficient—but not rigid and inflexible—and be patient enough to make sure positioning is complete before pushing for a sale.

ACTION PROJECT

Positioning for the Sale

Super salespeople seem to close everyone they try to sell. This appears to imply a 1:1 closing ratio. As a matter of fact, that is close to the truth. Even if they have interviews with many prospects each week, they only attempt to sell/close those for which they feel they are properly positioned. Getting to that point may take five minutes or five interviews. World-class salespeople have learned it pays in both time expended and money earned to position the prospect prior to attempting a close.

People buy what they want. Trying to power someone into a sale before they are ready loses sales and creates tension with a potential future client or a possible source of additional prospects.

With close friends or existing clients a good part of positioning has already been achieved in prior visits. But for this exercise let's assume you are meeting a potential client for the first time. The skill and techniques that follow should be utilized, at least in part, on every sales interview with both new and already known prospects.

Anatomy of the Sale

The successful sales effort generally incorporates five distinct subsales. The first four position you for the sale.

1. Sell yourself.
2. Sell your expertise.
3. Identify the prospect's needs or unfulfilled wants.
4. Propose a mutually acceptable solution or benefit.
5. Sell your specific product or service.

World-Class Selling

Consistent with the five parts of the sale, the actual sales procedure is also divided into five parts. Both the sale and the sales procedure are achieved concurrently. The first four parts of the sales procedure are essential for positioning and must be completed before attempting the close—which is number five.

1. Uncover the prospect's wants, dreams or aspirations.
2. Find out what has been done to achieve them.
3. If there is an inadequate "in-place" solution, take the "dream" away.
4. Give back the prospect's dream by showing a way to solve the problem.
5. Sell your proposed solution using your product or service.

Number of Interviews

We have not suggested the actual number of required interviews necessary to complete the sale. The number of interviews is a function of many circumstances. The whole process can be completed in one interview or after dozens. The best salespeople realize time is money so they never rush the selling interviews. On the other hand, they move to the point of positioning as quickly as possible and, if time allows, proceed immediately through to the close.

You have learned about the non-interview, the fact-finding interview and the closing interview. Though that implies that three interviews are required to complete the sales process, in actual practice all three interviews can be done at the same time. Some of the factors that determine the number of sales interviews required are:

- The amount of quality time available for each interview
- The location of interview and outside distractions
- The complexity of sale and the need for additional sale-related or product information
- The importance of the sale and the need to tread extra softly
- The salesperson's level of expertise and the need for outside assistance

- A frigid or negative prospect who requires a more personal touch
- The personality of the agent and his effectiveness in a slow, high-touch, presale relationship
- Other decision-makers who must be involved

During the positioning part of the sales process never argue, confront, challenge or try to change the mind of the prospect. You must learn what the prospect is trying to achieve. When you have an agreement on the problem and a benefit, nonproduct solution, you are ready to begin a sales close. If done properly and completely, any interview that gets that far is a highly probable sale if you close correctly.

In sales interviews there are times to listen and times to speak. Don't just listen with your ears. Use your eyes, mind and heart as well. Positioning means feeling what the prospect is trying to achieve as it relates to your product or service. Show an emotional and practical understanding of the problem and then get a consensus as to how it could be if the problem were solved (benefit statement).

If you don't do what you just learned in the next day or two, you'll probably never do it. Begin to practice the skills necessary to position yourself with every interview, starting right now.

The following schematic breaks the process down into three interviews and identifies the positioning parts and the direct sale parts.

Remember this can actually be accomplished in as few as one or as many interviews as necessary.

Also, do not begin 4 and 5 unless you are positioned to complete the sales process on that interview. If that is not the case, stop at 3 and schedule another interview to come back with a recommended solution to their problem.

Schematic of Sales Prospecting

Interview	Anatomy	Sale Procedure
Non-interview	1. Sell self	1a. Listen and learn— dreams, wants, aspirations of prospects.
	2. Sell expertise	1b. Prove competence by exploring what they want in areas relating to your product or services.
Finding the problem interview	3. Determine need/want ——————— Disturb	2. Find out what they have (and have not) done to achieve their objectives. 3. If there is a gap, take away their complacency.
End of Positioning	**Start of Close**	
Closing interview	4. Solution— benefit statement	4. Give back dream by suggesting there is a solution—get agreement on generic solution.
	5. Sell product/ service	5. Sell specific product/ service

10 | Making the Sale

J.1: AN OVERVIEW

Now that you're positioned, closing the sale might require nothing more than a demand for action such as: "Mr. Prospect, here's what we are going to do."

If that doesn't work some discussion may be in order—but only if it's really necessary. If the prospect doesn't buy, there's a chance that the sales process was not done properly, which makes closing impossible. We must learn to be objective about the entire procedure. We must take charge, be enthusiastic and be an implied-consent closer. If there is resistance, review mentally the first four parts of the sales process.

You may have failed to sell yourself, or your expertise, or you didn't find an unfulfilled dream or want, or you didn't convince the prospect of your ability to provide a solution to his or her problem.

If you were properly positioned on these four points, you'd be in a better position to favorably conclude a sale. The key word here is positioned. Great salespeople have learned to position themselves before attempting to sell a product so their closing ratios are extremely high.

209

Even with positioning, sales skills are necessary and the concepts in this section address many of those techniques.

The most successful salespeople have also learned that their own self-confidence, positive mental attitude, enthusiasm, knowledge, belief and communication skills are important requirements for success.

J.2: CLOSING

Before I discuss specific techniques, there are two critical points in closing that must be addressed:

1. Technically, closing is consummating the deal. It really begins when the salesperson first meets the prospect. If the prospect does not buy the salesperson, company, products, ideas or services, he might sit through a sales interview to be polite, but he's already decided not to buy.

2. To attempt to make a sale without properly positioning yourself significantly reduces the probability of a successful close.

Both of these areas are covered in many different ways within the covers of this book so this particular concept will concern itself only with what happens after the two above-referenced points are successfully achieved.

Presuming an open mind on the part of the prospect to the salesperson and the products he represents; and presuming the salesperson has done a good job positioning himself, it's time to get some action.

While the multiple closing strategies covered in this chapter can be done in any sequence, every close should begin with implied consent.

Implied Consent

If the prospect has been properly positioned, there is an awareness that a problem exists and a solution is needed. However, a direct question as to whether the prospect wants to buy opens the door to all kinds of problems. Super salespeople have learned to presume the prospect has decided to buy. It helps to believe the prospect has already said yes.

Therefore, the first step is not to ask whether the prospect wants to buy, but rather to take positive action. It's gentle persuasion, never with a club. The salesperson proceeds with whatever process is necessary to implement the sale, depending on the product. A certain number of prospects are, in fact, ready to buy at that point. For that group, if you say anything else you're more likely to hurt the sale than make it. Complete the order and leave.

Obviously, a significant number are not ready to move that fast and are likely to express some objection or ask some questions. We will discuss the techniques for handling those situations later. Just remember, implied consent is your first strategy. As a matter of fact, from that point forward, regardless of the number of objections, excuses and questions, the salesperson should complete each response with an implied consent type of action—as if the prospect had actually said, "Okay, let's proceed."

Fatal Alternatives

This is an implied consent action. As a basic sales principle the one asking questions is on the offense and in charge; the one answering is on the defense.

Whenever the salesperson makes a statement during the closing interview, it should often be followed with a fatal alternative question which offers two or more different choices. Though none can be answered with a simple yes or no, any direct response is a green light for a sale. Sample, fatal alternative questions could be:

- Would you rather pay for the whole order now or just give me a deposit?

- Do you want just 50 or would you prefer to have 100 because it's cheaper that way?

- Would you rather they be delivered to your home or your office?

Take Action

This is another implied consent strategy. Instead of asking questions, start filling out an order form. If you need a check, hand the prospect a pen and tell him or her the amount for which it should be written.

Just do something.

Remember, you finish every comment during the closing interview with an implied consent demand.

Yes, But

This is not an implied consent strategy, but it is a way to answer an objection, which then allows you to get back to implied consent. No matter what the prospect says to delay the sale—"I want to think about it," "I want to speak to my controller," "Please give me something in writing"—don't respond. Most of those are stalling tactics.

The best initial approach is to all but ignore the question and get right back to implied consent by using the yes/but technique. Here is an example of a yes/but response.

If the prospect says "Please give me something in writing," the response might be, "Of course, I always give my clients a complete written presentation. But in order to get the price I've quoted and timely delivery, let's get the order form completed first. Did you say you wanted this shipped to your home or to your office?"

Although you haven't actually used the words "yes, but," this demonstrates the "yes, but" technique, followed by the fatal alternative question presuming implied consent.

Excuse Versus Reason

Most people want to procrastinate. They want time to think your proposition over but that's just another way of saying no. If you don't complete the sale right then, there is a fair chance you never will. However, there is a good chance to sell if you close correctly.

In the course of a closing interview there may be many apparent objections, sometimes in rapid-fire order:

- I can't afford it.
- I want to speak to my accountant.
- I'd like something in writing.
- See me after the holidays.
- I'm too busy right now.

In most instances they don't mean any of those things, they're simply stalling, which is normal. When I plan on making a major purchase I do the same thing.

A good salesperson recognizes these are excuses, not reasons. They also realize they wouldn't be getting those kinds of excuses if the prospect wasn't somewhat interested and very close to buying. They'd get an out-and-out rejection. Procrastination is not evil, it's natural. Top salespeople have become experts at overcoming excuses. This is accomplished with self-confidence, implied consent, implementing the techniques of yes/but, asking for action and fatal alternatives—while bypassing the excuses.

Here are a few rebuttals:

- I certainly understand your concern.
- We will accommodate that situation.

- Let's at least get the paperwork completed.
- Where do you want this merchandise delivered? Then proceed with closing attempts.

Objections

Obviously, there are real objections to buying but they're more difficult to recognize. They start out sounding like another excuse. However, when there isn't a large variety of different excuses and the same one is repeated, there's a fair chance that if you don't answer, you're not going to make the sale. The two reasons weaker salespeople have trouble with objections are: (1) they overrespond to an excuse they misidentify as an objection; (2) they think an objection is a no.

Both are wrong.

Once you correctly identify a real objection, you should know that the prospect wants to buy but has a problem. If you can solve that problem you have a sale. In other words, an objection is really a yes!

The amazing thing is that most objections provide their own answer. For example, "I can't afford it" means "I can afford less than you're asking for. What are my other options?"

You can either sell them fewer of the same product, switch to a cheaper product or spread the payments, and you will probably make a sale.

Another example: "I want to speak to my accountant or my financial officer." Then say, "Let's set up an appointment with your accountant immediately."

Another might be: "I want to check the marketplace." Answer with, "I don't blame you, I would, too. If you tell me the companies you'd like quotes from, I'd be happy to do your shopping for you." (The way you respond to that objection would be somewhat influenced by your company and product limitations.)

Objections are not difficult to answer. With a positive mental attitude, with each answer followed with implied consent action, you will get many more successfully completed sales.

Reinforcing the Problem

If there is a great deal of resistance to your sales efforts, there's a chance you have either overestimated the prospect's problem or didn't adequately disturb the prospect.

The other possibility is you didn't get agreement on finding a solution. Rather than trying to overpower the prospect, this is the time to listen. Review the problem, the degree of disturbance and the great advantage of finding a solution. If you can get verbal agreement, try to close the sale. If not, find a real problem or leave. Without a prospect "want," a sale is nearly impossible.

Why?

Actually, Why? is only one of many questions that can be asked when the salesperson is losing a sale. If what the prospect is saying doesn't seem to make sense, in light of what has transpired during the positioning of the interview, it may be time to shift the pressure back to the prospect and go on the offense by asking questions.

Why? fits almost any situation. When the prospect's attitude isn't consistent with the earlier positioning, Why? followed by silence can be quite effective.

Silence

When the salesperson reaches a point of frustration and doesn't know what to do next, there is little to lose and everything to gain by increasing the pressure. The highest form of pressure is silence.

It can be preceded with Why? or it can be after a statement such as, "I'm utterly frustrated because I don't understand why, in light of everything we've discussed, you've chosen not to do anything about the problem."

Then remain mum. The first one that talks loses. Seconds seem like minutes, minutes seem like hours, but remain silent. It's a game of chicken.

Even after the prospect starts talking, don't respond. Eventually you may hear something that is the key to why no action has been taken; then you begin your sales effort all over again.

Motivating Stories

Depending on your product, most salespeople have stories to tell about something bad that happened because no action was taken, or something good that happened because it was.

After a while you have a portfolio of personal experiences that can apply to almost any situation. Until you develop a portfolio of your own, there are usually lots of stories available in your own company, or certainly within your industry, that are true—even if they happened to someone else. In any case, when all else fails, turn up the high-touch thermostat with personal motivation. Using specific emotional illustrations is often all you need to consummate a sale.

In practice the above techniques are much broader than implied herein. There are dozens of approaches but good salespeople just need a clue. Then, through practice and experimentation, they develop their own style to achieve the desired results.

If you haven't gotten there yet practice, practice. Have the courage to use implied consent as many times as the prospect says NO, plus one.

One last caution. Great salespeople are never overly aggressive, offensive or obnoxious, and earn the sale with gentle persuasion. A good friend of mine, who has since passed on, once said, "I know a lot of you want to hear how I became successful at selling, but I have a confession. I have never made a sale in my entire life."

After the audience had time to react to this unexpected statement he broke into a big grin and said, "But I have taken a great many orders."

The highest compliment I get from new clients is when they thank me and then say they appreciate the fact that I didn't push them into buying but helped them solve a problem.

Struggling salespeople feel like they are always in the middle of a fight. With gentle persuasion, people thank you and your sales will improve dramatically.

J.3: DON'T BELIEVE IT

Salespeople tend to listen to the objections they get from their prospects. In the early days of their career they tend to believe them all.

As a consumer I've gone into automobile salesrooms, television dealerships and other retail outlets. Even though I might be interested in buying, I'll usually say, "I'm just looking." Sometimes I say, "I'd never buy anything without talking to my wife."

Why do we do this?

No one wants to be trapped into buying something until they are ready. And most of us don't like saying no to a salesperson.

I don't think people are bad for telling small lies like this. But I've learned not to take them at their word.

Early in my career I was trying to sell a life insurance policy to one of my closest friends. I knew he desperately needed it and I felt he could afford it. He and his wife were a young couple with a growing family and a house with a large mortgage, but they were living very well. In those days I sold all kinds of insurance, not just life insurance, and I was already taking care of their fire and automobile coverage.

I had dinner at their home and the sales interview began immediately thereafter. It was still going strong at 11:00 P.M. At that time the husband took out his checkbook to show me he had a negative balance and brought out a stack of unpaid bills that would have choked a horse.

They finally convinced me that they couldn't afford the life insurance. I gave up and left.

A week later my telephone rang. It was my good friend asking me to get a casualty insurance floater on the new mink coat he had just bought for his wife. I was nonplussed. With appropriate restraint I took the order and didn't mention the negative bank balance.

It was one of the greatest sales lessons I've ever had. I eventually completed the life insurance sale, but never completely believed a prospect again.

People buy what they want to buy. That means they may fabricate a story to avoid buying what they don't want. Be aware of that fact without using it against them. Instead, when you get procrastination or excuses, try to find a stronger incentive for them to buy what you're selling. Help them achieve something important and avoid being confrontational at all costs.

J.4: SELLING THE WANT

Most people don't buy what they need, they buy what they want.

A close friend of mine once indicated that he wanted to purchase some insurance on his young child. I convinced the family, over their strong objections, that the money would be better spent by extending the parent's life insurance protection. Consummating that very difficult sale, I left feeling satisfied with what I had done.

Some months later, while visiting the family, I noticed a premium statement from another insurance company. I asked them about it. Embarrassed, they explained that when I wouldn't sell it to them they had bought the juvenile insurance from another agent. I learned a valuable lesson that day.

It is extremely important to hear the things that concern the prospect. Listening to the tone of the prospect's voice can give you more information than what is expressed by words. Train yourself to hear the dreams, frustrations, business and personal needs, fears and desires. They will give you a clue to what problems must be solved in order to sell.

It is essential that you clearly establish the wants of the prospect and not transfer your own standards and values. We all have different approaches to life. We are not all equally motivated.

Be careful to design the solution to fulfill the prospect's wants, not yours.

J.5: WHAT IS "NO"?

Many salespeople, particularly new ones, don't recognize a "no" when they hear one. They hear a lot of "maybe's," which gives them hope. It is usually a false hope because it was really a "no" disguised as a "maybe."

Here are some thoughts to help recognize a "no."

- Anything other than a completed sale is a "no," whether you believe it or not.

- Even with a "maybe," chances are the power of the salesperson will erode with subsequent interviews. It would have been better to go for the sale immediately; it was probably your best chance.

- A prospect who is communicating "maybe's" may require so many interviews that it won't be cost efficient in the long run. Therefore, get rid of the "maybe's." Go for a definite "yes" or "no."

- Most people are too nice to say "no" outright. Therefore, you are more likely to get a "maybe," a postponement or an excuse. Anything other than a sale is a "no."

These areas are the shades of gray. They're not absolute, they're probabilities. If you are positioned to make a sale, anything other than an order is a "no."

There are exceptions so this is not an absolute rule. If the sale is large enough, and your relationship is strong, on occasion you may want to extend the sales effort with additional interviews. Just be selective when you make that decision. In all other situations *go for it now!*

J.6: KEEP-IT-SIMPLE PROPOSALS

The KISS formula (Keep It Simple Stupid) and my Levine Formula (the fatter the proposal, the stupider the salesperson) are very important concepts. Actually they both are strong reasons for a heavy emphasis on education.

It's harder to make a good five-minute speech than one that takes an hour. Likewise, amateurs make easy things look difficult, pros make difficult things look easy.

Uneducated salespeople are inclined to answer every possible question in a long written proposal since they fear being asked something they don't know. By providing more information than is necessary to make the sale, they are introducing dozens of questions and objections that the prospect never would have thought to ask. In addition, the length and complexity of the presentation will bore the prospect and is likely to kill the probability of a sale.

Well-trained, well-educated salespeople can sell effectively using a paper napkin, a yellow pad, an easel or at most a one-pager—provided they know their business and can answer any question thrown at them.

Education is not to make simple situations complicated, but to make all situations simple. A proposal should only make the points necessary to make the sale; it should be as brief as possible.

J.7: PROTECTING WHOSE SENSIBILITIES?

After a half century in the selling business, I still feel pressure when the deal begins to close. It is a moment of excitement. Selling is as stimulating now as it was the day I started. Although it sometimes is tempting to walk out and run away from the pressure, I enjoy the challenge.

Many salespeople leave too soon. They allow themselves to be brushed off too easily.

Why do so many leave at that time rather than staying and getting the job done?

Most of the rationalizations are:

- I don't want to be an obnoxious bore.
- I don't want to be seen as an aggressive salesman.
- I don't want to turn the prospect off.
- I want the prospect to like me.

If we really have our prospects' best interests in mind, if we know they need our product, we would not leave until we have done everything in our power to improve their situation.

The reason we leave is not to avoid offending the sensibilities of the prospect. We leave because we are afraid of abusing or offending our own sensibilities. We are being self-protective. We want to maintain our own false pride. It seems quite obvious that true pride is realized by attaining the level of success that we wish for ourselves.

We must set our goals and objectives, establish our motivation, then go out and pay the price. For some it's a very high price indeed.

ACTION PROJECT

Making the Sale

If closing the sale has been your problem, from now on, when a sales effort ends in a "no" or a "maybe," use the following checklist to determine what you may have done wrong.

Presuming the salesperson has effectively positioned the sales interview (see chapter 9 and action project "Positioning for the Sale"), the so-called closing of the sale can usually be successfully achieved by using techniques based upon implied consent.

In other words—if the prospect has become comfortable with the salesperson, if the prospect has accepted the salesperson's competence and expertise, if the prospect has agreed that he or she has an unfulfilled want (or problem), and if the prospect has agreed that the salesperson can provide a benefit (solution) that will fulfill the wants (or solve the problem) that the prospect has acknowledged is of great concern, and finally, if the prospect has implied he or she is interested in implementing a solution, then the salesperson is positioned for the close and implied consent should work. Of course even without being completely "positioned," a certain number of closing attempts will be successful. As a matter of fact, I've worked with thousands of salespeople and I have never seen one so bad he couldn't sell something to somebody, and, conversely, I have never seen one so good he could sell anything to everybody.

All that world-class selling techniques can do for the salesperson is improve the ratios. Presuming the same number of sales attempts, the resulting number of sales achieved will be heavily influenced by the skill level of the salesperson.

Of course, the quality of the prospect and the competitive cost and quality of the product will also affect the salesperson's effectiveness, but all things being equal, sales skills will significantly impact sales results.

In that context, this "making the sale" project is an exercise to improve sales ratios. The salesperson must realize part of success is being mentally prepared for getting lots of rejection but also starting each close enthusiastically expecting a sale.

Also, the salesperson must remember effectiveness is greatly influenced by all the steps taken before attempting the close. The sale actually begins even before the prospect is contacted for the first time.

A list of contributing factors for sales success or the lack thereof would include all of the following and you should score yourself for each factor. Those "to be addressed" should be monitored and implemented immediately.

	Okay	To Be Addressed
• The salesperson's general appearance	_____	_____
• The quality of the salesperson's product/service	_____	_____
• The cost of the product	_____	_____
• The quality of the prospect	_____	_____
Ability to pay?		
Urgency of need for product/service?		
Ability to see prospect under favorable circumstances?		
• The power of salesperson/prospect relationship	_____	_____

Personal contact?
Strong referral? } Stronger
Existing client?

Cold canvass?
Direct mail? } Weaker
Etc.

	Okay	To Be Addressed
• The effectiveness at getting a good appointment	_____	_____

Review and score your sales attempts.

	Did This	Next Time
• The "positioning of the sale"		
Selling salesperson's "self"?	_____	_____
Selling salesperson's expertise?	_____	_____
Developing want of prospect?	_____	_____
Getting significant relevant facts?	_____	_____
Discovering unfulfilled want?	_____	_____
Disturbing prospect by taking away their want?	_____	_____
Offering solution to the problem?	_____	_____
Getting general acceptance of desire for solution	_____	_____

and finally . . .

• Closing the sale!

When a sale is not consummated, and there is no obvious reason for the failure, look back at the above list and honestly critique your positioning before you blame your closing technique. What are prospects' potential reasons for not buying? Even if there is no reason not to buy, the sale can still be lost if the salesperson fails to get the prospect to take action, now!

The closing process will include as many of the following techniques as are necessary to take action and complete the sale.

Implied Consent/Initiate Action—If properly positioned, presume and act as if the prospect said "yes," so take sales-related action. Fill out order—tell the prospect what we will do now.

Did _____   Didn't do _____   Need practice _____

Fatal Alternatives—Don't ask closing questions that can be answered with a "no." Example: "Would you like to proceed with the sale?"—rather say, "Do you want to pay the whole price now or just give me a deposit?"

Did _____   Didn't do _____   Need practice _____

Yes—But . . .—Never get into a direct confrontation with the prospect. No matter what he says, answer his challenge with weak agreement but then share your perspective. Example: Prospect says "I can get it for less money." Answer, "Perhaps, but there is no product that can do all the things you want as well as mine can" (Yes, but.)

Did _____   Didn't do _____   Need practice _____

Questions—Anytime the salesperson is losing control of the situation, ask questions. It buys you time and puts you on offense and the prospect on defense. There are lots of questions but "Why?" is a great one.

Did _____   Didn't do _____   Need practice _____

Silence—When the prospect hasn't given a good reason not to buy, but you sense there is something on his mind, ask a question and keep quiet for a long time. First one to talk loses.

Did _____   Didn't do _____   Need practice _____

Motivating Stories—If the interview bogs down, review the problem you are trying to solve and put some sizzle into the interview by telling motivating stories about similar situations in which solutions were or were not implemented, and the results therefrom.

Did _____   Didn't do _____   Need practice _____

Excuses—Most of the things the prospect says to avoid taking action "now" are excuses, not reasons. A prospect will bring up lots of excuses for delaying action that are really not significant. Answer all procrastination—so-called reasons—with a "yes, but" response and keep on closing.

Did _____   Didn't do _____   Need practice _____

Real Objections—If the same excuse comes up over and over again, it might be a real objection to buying and must be answered. I suggest if it comes up in the same form more than three times, it should not be ignored. Remember, however, most objections are not a "no" to the sale but rather a "yes" under certain conditions. For example, if the objection is "I can't afford it," the prospect is really saying "I want it but I don't know how to pay for it." All you have to do is either find the money (often cost savings) or find a less expensive product. Either way, you have a sale.

Did _____   Didn't do _____   Need practice _____

Multiple Closes—Once you begin the close, end everything you say with either:
  • A demand for action (such as filling out an order)

                                  or

  • A fatal alternative question (such as, "Will you pay for it all or just a deposit?").

Did _____   Didn't do _____   Need practice _____

No matter which of the above techniques you are using (yes—but . . . , motivating stories, etc.), end with another close.

I once heard a great salesperson say, "You should always attempt to close as many times as the prospect says no, plus one." My experience has conclusively proven most salespeople don't try to close often enough and quit too soon.

After a closing interview when the sale attempt fails, review the above list of techniques and see if you really used all the skills you had available. If not, be sure to review them again before your next close and don't make the same mistake twice.

11

Client Services

K.1: AN OVERVIEW

All clients are customers but all customers are not clients. Clients are people with whom you do business but with whom you also developed a strong interpersonal business relationship.

Thus, the client feels comfortable calling on your expertise, when needed. Likewise, you are comfortable knowing you can visit the client for a private interview at almost any time.

How does a customer become a client?

Most consumers buy products. Period. They don't develop a relationship with the company or its representative. If they accidentally ran into their representative, they could pass by with no recognition whatsoever. If you are a salesperson there are many situations when spending more than just a short time on the sales process might be counterproductive. However, if you want to build a lifetime career in selling, converting customers to clients who are loyal to you is very important.

Actually developing clients is mutually beneficial. The client knows the salesperson will deliver future services and is available whenever needed; the salesperson knows the client is open to new products or services and can be called upon.

Even in retail stores where a large volume of shoppers is the rule and client relationships rare, good salespeople have learned to develop long-term client ties with their steady customers.

The sale isn't the end, it's the beginning. All promises made at the point of sale should be fulfilled ahead of time and, if possible, exceeded. Frequent contacts in person, through the mail and on the phone are essential, and regular contacts and updates are all part of the process.

You have to work a little harder to make a customer a client but not only is it more fun, it is significantly more rewarding. As your client base grows, you grow and many more doors will be opened through the referred lead process. Client services may not be the easiest and fastest way to earned commissions, but in the long run, they are the secret to increased earnings and a long-term career.

K.2: WHAT IS A CLIENT?

Obviously, for an accountant, attorney, or some other special business relationship requiring regular ongoing service, most business relationships are client relationships.

However, for the salesperson, when the sale has been made, you have a new customer. You have earned your commission and the prospect has solved a problem.

For ordinary salespeople that completes the sales cycle. For world-class salespeople this begins a relationship.

An analogy of the concepts in this chapter can be found in the game of pool. You cannot be a champion pool player if you only put the correct ball in the pocket. You must also make sure the cue ball is in a position that sets up the next shot. Only if you can sustain a series of successful shots can you excel at pool.

Selling follows that same pattern. You can make a living on individual sales by working extra hard. To be a champion you must make the one-time customer into a lifetime client from whom you can anticipate future sales, referrals and testimonials. Doing this is a skill that is often overlooked.

It begins with developing a trusting, caring, sharing interpersonal relationship (see chapter 9). Next, this alliance is enhanced by selling quality products and/or services in an ethical and professional manner—while helping the client solve a personal or business problem (see chapter 10). Finally, the post-sale effort giving extra service and value-added benefits solidifies the client-agent relationship.

Good salespeople figure out early in their career that their most valuable business asset is their client inventory. The objective, which is a major key to success, is to develop a large inventory of valuable clients. When you have enough established clients so that your personal sales goals can be achieved by simply servicing and selling existing clients and the prospects they refer to you, you have reached a point of perpetual success with minimal effort.

For example, some products—such as razors, mobile phone systems, business machines and photographic film—are sold under cost as loss leaders because the products and/or services needed to use them develop a guaranteed future flow of sales— razor blades, phone service, paper and supplies, developing and processing.

Many automobile dealers discount new car sales to marginal profit levels to get future service and repair services, which generate high revenue.

Commission salespeople can achieve the same long-term results because of client relationships. Post-sale service is a simple, pleasant way to work smarter instead of harder.

K.3: THAT'S *MY* CLIENT

It's not unusual for a salesperson to discover that someone they perceived to be a good friend or an existing client also buys similar products and services from other business people.

While many salespeople provide service in diverse areas, or represent a broad variety of products, that doesn't mean their clients will buy exclusively from them.

Just because you sold a product doesn't make the purchaser a client. Such a presumption generates a false sense of security. It is not unlikely that other salespeople, representing similar or comparable skills, services and products, may also have sold the customer. They, too, consider that purchaser to be their client.

Many superior salespeople approach the same prospects. This tends to drive the more passive salesperson out of the picture.

What can be done to protect you from losing people you consider good prospects or clients?

Let me suggest some possibilities:

- Determine which product lines and services are appropriate for you and your market. Then broaden your product portfolio. Educate yourself. Develop the appropriate skills to impress your clients and prospects with your expertise.

- Be sure to remind your prospects and clients, through mailing and personal interviews, about your total product and service portfolio.

- Go to every client regularly and explain your total portfolio, particularly in the areas you have not previously addressed. Try to eliminate competition (even if someone else was there first) by taking over that service or sale.

- Develop working relationships with other salespeople with compatible products and services you can't sell, or choose not to sell, and have them service your clients in those areas to keep out competition. Expect reciprocity.

In client relationships it is important that the client is aware of all your products and services and considers you his value-added professional salesperson.

K.4: CARING REVIEWS

In my early selling years, it bothered me when I'd suggest getting together with a prospect and the response was, "I'm not ready to buy anything else right now."

Customers are touchy. They think every visit is another attempt to make a sale.

Fine salespeople deliver value-added service and know that high touch is more important than high tech. They also know that clients think the only time a salesperson knocks is when he wants to make a sale. Regardless of the true motives of the salesperson, perception is reality. I don't care what product line you represent, your clients deserve your high-touch attention when it's not motivated by commission dollars. Be sure your customer knows it. At the very least there should be periodic reviews and visits—not less than once a year.

Those visits should be to touch base, keep in touch, see if there's anything you can do to help. This type of visit is a far better use of time than sitting in the office and playing prospect solitaire when there is no one to see. At the very least you should come away with referred leads.

Even if you get nothing, you're reinforcing your relationship with the client. Further, the client is less likely to be defensive every time you visit which makes future sales attempts more pleasant.

The client's perception should be that you care and the visits are sincere. Therefore, in your weekly, monthly and annual planning, see to it that every client has one or two visits a year, scheduled in advance, for no other purpose than to touch base.

Some of those visits will end with sales. Of course, besides these service/social type visits there should be occasional reviews to make sure that the product you sold is still effective. Perhaps there is a need for other sales. You should, therefore, schedule two kinds of visits each year: those specifically geared at sales and service, and those specifically geared for strengthening interpersonal relationships.

My personal experience has proven that this type of activity is positive and constructive. It is definitely worth the extra time and effort it requires.

K.5: NEWSLETTERS, BROCHURES AND CARDS

Most successful people have some automated systems to assure regular communication with business-related people on a year-round basis.

There is no one right way to accomplish this mission but some attention to this broad area of communications is appropriate for all business people. The following items are some of the materials and systems I use.

Brochures

Depending on your business, clientele and credentials, decide if a brochure is appropriate and, if so, how expansive it should be. It can be a one-page résumé or a multi-page, color brochure with graphics.

Many companies provide brochures that are adequate for their representatives and sometimes they can be customized and personalized with pictures, names, addresses and phone numbers. An attractive business card is essential, but it might be quite valuable to also have a descriptive piece that promotes your individual competence, expertise, products and services. It can be used as part of an initial mail contact, as a handout when you meet someone for the first time, or simply as an alternative to the calling card.

Newsletters

I have always used monthly newsletters. I've written my own and I've bought them from franchise services. Some have had my picture printed on the front, others have simply had the name, address and phone number somewhere in the text. At least once a month my existing clients and all my current hot prospects receive a newsletter with information I hope they find interesting. Frankly, it is only on rare occasions when the substance of the newsletter created direct business. On the other hand, it has kept my name in front of people. For my business it is both time and cost effective to buy a prepared franchise piece and have my assistant automatically handle the mailings.

Greeting Cards

I have a completely automated system for sending out cards for special occasions. Every one of my clients, associates and some high-quality prospects receives a birthday card from me, personally signed, sometimes with a single fresh flower. I also use calendars and greeting cards for the holiday season and a much larger list receives a greeting from me at the end of every year.

I've tried to find items that are different and uniquely me. For example, I have a small, attractive, wildlife calendar (most people know of my love of nature) that I send out in lieu of a greeting card to 500 special people. I frequently receive either verbal or written comments of appreciation. When I have, on occasion, dropped somebody from the calendar list and run into them at some social function, it's not uncommon for them to say there must have been a mistake because they didn't get my calendar. Of course, I immediately send them one and put them back on the list. All greeting cards are personalized. I use a calligrapher to address the calendars and they are sent with real stamps. It's the personal touch that counts.

Commercial Calendars

I also send hundreds of desk calendars to some of the same people, at least one month before the holiday greeting cards.

My experience has been that the first calendars received are the ones that get used, and when others arrive they are usually trashed. I have some corporate clients that like them so much, they ask me to send an additional 15 or 20 so they can give them to each of their employees for their office desks.

Gifts

Gifts are used on a much more selective basis. For my best clients and key associates I have two basic types of gifts. I give a select few a leather pocket diary with their initials inscribed on the cover which they use as their datebook for the entire year. For others I give a two-bottle boxed wine selection with a label imprinted with "Chosen for your special pleasure by Sandy and Norman Levine." These are hand delivered to special people when I visit them.

I deliberately overstock so that during the year, for social or courtesy visits, I bring along a wine gift box instead of buying flowers or candy. To send good wishes because of illness or accident I send teddy bears with bandages on the appropriate body location and a card that says "teddy hugs" from Norman and Sandy.

In any instance, brochures, newsletters, appropriate greeting cards and gifts are an important part of my interpersonal communication activities. I have illustrated this concept with some of my own systems hoping they may trigger some ideas for you on how to create a program of your own.

K.6: SUCCESSORS

In a world of "what have you done for me lately" or "how fast they forget," concerned business people must worry about their clientele, and their potential economic value, when he or she is no longer around. We have all seen the lifetime efforts of ethical business people quickly disappear, or worse, aggressively exploited by scavengers who pounce on the residual pot of gold when the business person dies or retires.

For salespeople, as for all business people, at death or retirement, many prime clients are targets for less professional salespeople. Very few companies will protect these valuable orphan clients from their own perhaps unscrupulous, aggressive salespeople. There are two reasons: (1) they fear estranging active sales reps who want orphaned clients, and (2) they want all the business they can get, by any means available.

There are thousands of stories of feeding frenzies. Many successful salespeople are struggling to seek some foolproof method to insure the survival and well-being of their life's work after their death or retirement. In some cases, because of company control, it may be impossible to achieve.

Good intentions have only rarely proven effective. From the point of view of the client, the former salesperson (if there are residual commissions) and the company, the answer is a guaranteed transfer system. This would allow the intelligent choice of a qualified and dedicated successor. It would certainly be good for everyone if we could provide a successorship program that might include:

1. A mentor program to encourage successful salespeople to help recruit, and/or train, and/or develop a mentor/protégé relationship with promising candidates.

2. Business structures, perhaps a corporation, wherein the existing and future clientele are assigned to a group of two or more salespeople who are co-owners of the business.

3. A close partnership, formal or informal, whereby clients learn to respect and feel comfortable with two or more salespeople so client control is not lost if one of the salespeople dies or retires. This client control is stronger than any contract.

Of course, depending on your company, product, service or compensation, these ideas may be totally inappropriate. However, in other situations they may provide a great opportunity for protecting the results of a lifetime career.

Whether you are a salesperson or not, a professional practice continuation plan is good for everyone involved and your customers or clients should be assured of continuous service indefinitely.

ACTION PROJECT

Client Services

The objective of this project is to develop interpersonal relationships so that every buyer becomes a client. The following
checklist is not all-inclusive but lists many of the standard procedures that may contribute to this mission. Identify those
things you are doing and sustain them. Identify those you are
not doing and implement them.

	Doing	Not Doing	Implement
• Prospect and client file system to trigger contacting and service scheduling.	_____	_____	_____
• Annual, or more frequent, client reviews.	_____	_____	_____
• Schedule occasional nonsale-related client visits.	_____	_____	_____
• Regular newsletter.	_____	_____	_____
• Holiday greeting cards.	_____	_____	_____
• Birthday and/or event cards.	_____	_____	_____
• Client gifts.	_____	_____	_____
• Calendars.	_____	_____	_____
• Social visitations.	_____	_____	_____
• Product and service update bulletins.	_____	_____	_____
• Complete comprehensive file for every client available to an assistant or business associate in an emergency.	_____	_____	_____

	Doing	Not Doing	Implement
• Full-time coverage in your office when you are out.	_____	_____	_____
• A successor plan for your retirement, disability or death.	_____	_____	_____
• Establish client relationships with your assistant or associate for comfort and service when you are ill or on vacation.	_____	_____	_____
• Phone, fax and, perhaps, online communication equipment.	_____	_____	_____
• Build your own community presence and visibility to be a center of influence for clientele.	_____	_____	_____
• Have a public relations program on an ongoing basis.	_____	_____	_____
• Targeted advertising.	_____	_____	_____
• Be active—when possible in clubs or organizations that have a good nest of clients.	_____	_____	_____
• Share your success and awards with your clients so they know you are the best.	_____	_____	_____
• Schedule phone calls just to touch base with key prospects and clients at least quarterly.	_____	_____	_____
• Make sure all promises made at point of sale are kept or exceeded and ahead of time (have system to assure completion).	_____	_____	_____

Necessary client services vary from product to product, and from client to client. Nonetheless, world-class salespeople often have a flair for standing out from the crowd. Every salesperson should review the above list, consider other techniques that exist in his situation, then do more than his competition. We may be able to survive as salespeople by doing less, but to be world class we must each do more to stand apart.

12

Systems and Procedures

L.1: AN OVERVIEW

It's been said unsuccessful people don't know where they are going or how to get there. So they end up nowhere.

I don't know if that is true but I have known many unsuccessful ones who tried to reinvent the wheel every day. Even if they managed to avoid failure, they spend most of their energy wastefully. Sadly, they rarely improve.

On the other hand, successes develop standard operating procedures they use all the time. Interpersonal skills and effective communication are art forms. Practice, practice, practice makes perfect.

Can you imagine learning a skill in the classroom, then, without practice, attempting to perform before an audience?

Or picture a nondriver getting behind the wheel of a new car and taking it out onto the freeway. It would make more sense to have a few lessons with an experienced driver, as well as a basic knowledge of the fundamental rules of the road.

Our careers depend in large measure on working effectively and smarter, not harder. For efficiency's sake, all processes that can be standardized and/or delegated should be. Our unique skills should be used with organized, rehearsed procedures. Time control is essential for maximum productivity.

Systems and procedures are the link that completes the loop leading to success. This section will share many concepts that might help accelerate your effectiveness.

L.2: STANDARD OPERATING PROCEDURES

At a recent industry meeting, I shared some of my systems and procedures. In private one-on-one sessions I was amazed at the number of professional field people who do not have standard procedures for all business activities.

I found two predominant types:

1. Veterans who once had systems but who have since abandoned them in order to survive in today's environment. Now they are staying totally loose and flexible and have not reestablished standard procedures.

2. Younger people who never had systems and are building more or less on seat-of-the-pants strategies.

There is no question that adaptability and flexibility are key qualities in today's environment. However, building a successful life today is tough enough without making it tougher. Systems are more important than ever before. Some thoughts to reinforce these observations:

- Transferring an individual's skills to his support team— and to other associates—requires standard systems that do not depend on the person's unique skills and personality for successful implementation.

- Reinventing the wheel for each situation is a wasteful exercise; standard operating procedures can free time for creative endeavors.

- The training and educating of your personal and business teams require consistency and will not work if you change the rules or give mixed signals. The more boilerplate the procedures, the more efficient and cost effective you will be.

- Copy established systems from your company and your industry. They have valuable materials available that can provide the foundation for many programs and save you time.

- No one is forever. Building a thriving career and having it survive is the greatest tribute. Having someone else run your business while you are ill or traveling (or permanently because of death or retirement) demands standard, written procedures to make internal transitions more effective. Your associates and your clients deserve nothing less. And you have earned the right to take time off without feeling like you are cheating the business.

L.3: CANNED TALKS

Rarely does a successful salesperson use the company's sales talk exactly as it was taught. However, a word-for-word sales track is the quickest and best means to a successful career.

Sales managers are either obsessed with memorized perfection or so casual they don't even bother to teach a presentation. Both approaches are wrong.

New salespeople will usually resist a canned talk, but most need it. It is the fastest approach to a successful sales career, and should be sold to new recruits as a necessary means to an end. Eventually, they will earn the right to modify it and the presentation will begin to reflect his personality and preferences. In time it will become his trademark.

In situations where a strong, experienced salesperson is entering a new sales career, he might prefer to develop a presentation to fit his own personality. The resulting pitch should be based on the company's standard presentation and jointly prepared by the trainer or sales manager. In any instance, it is still a prepared, memorized sales track.

The bottom line is almost all truly successful people have standard procedures which they totally embrace and which they deliver over and over with power and confidence. These procedures may, over time, evolve into presentations that are uniquely theirs, but the presentations are still a rehearsed, organized approach. Most very successful speakers, politicians and business leaders develop a few basic speeches and do them over and over; they simply change the audience.

Only amateurs make up a presentation as they go along.

An indication that a new salesperson is not prepared to pay the price of success is his refusal to learn the standard talk because "it isn't him." Seat-of-the-pants sales pitches are for amateurs. World-class professionals learn, refine, practice and perform their presentations until they are so powerful and effective, they appear spontaneous.

L.4: RECORD KEEPING

Most driver-expressive personalities—and for that matter, most motivated people—find record keeping a burden and an inconvenience. Of course, there are some people who enjoy keeping records, but they are not in the majority.

Record keeping is the only way to accurately determine what is going right and what is going wrong. Most of us instinctively believe we know precisely what we're doing. When records are kept, we usually learn that our impressions were not even close to reality. The only sure way to know what, if anything, we should change is by the statistics of our past performance. For that reason, all salespeople should set up a precise record-keeping system.

It need not be burdensome, nor should it take a great deal of time. One half-hour planning session a week is probably enough.

Great successes also know where they've been, where they are now, where they're going and what must be done to get there.

For example, minimum records for salespeople should include:

- Income produced (and the sources).
- What money is being spent (and what it's being spent on).
- The levels of past activity (how many and what kind of prospects are being seen).
- The sources of past prospects.
- Which presentations were used.
- How many telephone calls have to be made in order to get one good interview (based on the source and type of person being called).
- How many closing interviews are needed to generate one sale.

- How much is earned from the sale.
- Which prospects and products represent the most effective income-producing sources.

If you are not a professional salesperson, similar essential functions should be recorded. In other words, set up a semi-automatic system that does all of the above. If you have an assistant, delegate.

Today there are many computer software packages available to help you keep records. In some industries, there are specialized custom-tailored packages to do it for you. At the very least get a generic one to save time and energy.

The real problem is that many people just don't want to do it. You can delegate this job to others, but you must completely understand it and be able to teach it yourself. To be effective, you must understand what information is needed and what to do with it.

Once the system is operational, at least on a quarterly basis, critique the numbers to determine where your skills are breaking down and where you are most successful. Use the concepts in this book if your assessment determines that part of your process is not effective.

For example, if you isolated just the part of record keeping that concentrates on activity and you wanted to determine if your time was being used effectively, you might look for the answers to the following questions:

- How many people am I seeing?
- Where did those people come from?
- When I contacted them, how effective was I at converting a contact to an interview?
- What percentage do I sell successfully?
- What is my income from the average interview?

Once you know the answers, you will also be able to identify the problems. You can then concentrate on eliminating the negatives and increasing the positives by utilizing your appropriate skill areas discussed in this book.

This is just an example of record keeping implemented and utilized for productivity. The point is you can track trends in every business which, when used for planning, will make you more effective.

If any of the trends are in the wrong direction, you should take action to determine what is wrong and how it can be fixed.

Record keeping separates amateurs from professionals, because pros get paid based on results.

L.5: FINANCIAL RECORD SYSTEMS

Apart of record keeping that people find inconvenient is maintaining expense records for tax and business purposes. I, too, was not very well-disciplined in that area, so I developed a system that works for me.

My assistant keeps a duplicate diary of every place I am going each day, and checks with me occasionally to confirm that nothing new has been added. I charge everything or I write checks. I avoid cash payments whenever possible. If I must use cash I get a receipt.

I have separated the credit cards into two types: (1) business and (2) personal. Two credit cards are used for business expenses; two different ones are used for personal expenses.

When I give my assistant a batch of receipts, he checks the date on the slip and his diary to determine who I entertained. He knows that if I used a business credit card, it is tax deductible. Otherwise, it is a personal expense. The only time this system breaks down is when an establishment will not take the appropriate card. Then I use cash and write down what the purpose was on the receipt.

Since establishing this relatively simple mechanical approach, I have kept better records. My assistant does most of the work, and his diary has proven quite complete for tax audit purposes. This system has an additional benefit: My assistant always knows where I am because of the duplicate diary. Anyone trying to reach me can contact my assistant who can make appointments for me in my absence.

For paying bills I have two bank accounts. One is personal; the other business. All bills are separated and are entered into the computer. Checks are issued and each item is automatically put into a ledger by category. Each month my accountant gets the ledgers for tax and budgeting controls. All of this takes a minimum of my time and the job is effectively maintained. The only breakdown is the occasional business-related cash expense item I forget to record. I take full responsibility for those mistakes but the price is less than the value of the time saved.

L.6: DELEGATION

The inability to delegate stems from the false belief that a person can do it better by himself, and in less time.

This is a delusion.

Even if the staff person to whom a task was delegated was less efficient initially, the time saved and the work accomplished more than justifies the assignment effort. Such delegation, even at an initial 50 percent capability means two employees will turn out as much work in their areas as the delegator. This leaves the delegator free to do more important and productive things. Also, the 50 percent will soon improve with training and experience. The question is what and how to delegate.

Consider these thoughts:

1. Delegation is the only way to grow really big.

2. Delegation without adequate training is counter-productive.

3. Delegate only that which others can eventually do as well as or better than you.

4. Don't delegate the things at which you excel—which, for the salesperson, means prospecting and selling.

5. Once an item is delegated, accept mistakes, but let your subordinate know you won't accept the same mistake twice.

6. Even if you think your subordinate is wrong, allow some leeway. If it doesn't work, presume it won't be done that way again, but refrain from saying, "I told you so." And always give credit where it is due.

7. If subordinates can't perform effectively under those conditions, replace them.

8. Do not delegate to a third line of command unless your second line is strong enough to implement the above items. Have them report to you on the progress of their subordinates.

Successful people get paid for results. Any time spent on anything else is counterproductive. Find a talented assistant to train. Have patience. As you then get additional discretionary time, use it to to achieve bottom line results. With such systems in place, the time and money an assistant requires will prove to be a fantastic investment.

L.7: STUDY GROUPS

Developing close interpersonal relationships with other successful people is very important. Many top people have joined study groups made up of other ambitious people.

Some of these groups meet just once a year, others once a month. They are usually peer groups of people committed to a common cause. It's not unusual to have total disclosure at these meetings as to income, contracts, circumstances, skills and techniques. In time, a strong bond of friendship develops as the group grows, prospers and matures.

Usually one or two members become highly successful, but as the bar is raised, every member gains and prospers. Even the lowest achievers in a great study group are usually among the top achievers in their industry.

Forming a study group is the challenge. Some industries have trade associations where people gather. This is a good place to meet others in your industry. From these meetings, friendships develop. If you want to form a study group it's usually not too difficult to get a half dozen or more people together— for work, play or a common cause. A group can consist of participants from a single company, or it can be varied with only one representative from each company.

The groups I belong to generally meet once a year and we divide all of the expenses including travel and accommodations equally among all of the participants. We anticipate 100 percent attendance at every meeting (except for catastrophes). We presume everything that's discussed will be kept confidential and is for the sole use of the members of the group. We've become extremely close friends and often contact each other for direction and assistance. On occasion, despite careful screening, someone gets in the group who isn't compatible or who doesn't have the same intense commitment. We reluctantly ask that person to leave. The group must have the courage to stand together as a whole, undivided.

Competition within the group is virtually nonexistent. We respect each other although some are more successful than others. Each of us has some great attributes so everyone is respected and admired. There is no hierarchy based on productivity.

I think study groups have a great place in any industry. They are a perfect vehicle for people who are dreaming bigger dreams than they are currently realizing.

Groups run between 5 and 12 members. But there's no magic in the structure or format. Most of my groups rotate a member host for each meeting and the other members travel to his location. This gives us a chance to see the host's environment. There is complete cost sharing, even by the one who didn't have to travel. Some groups occasionally meet in neutral territory or resort facilities. Meetings are work sessions so when spouses are invited, they are entertained by the host spouse. Evenings may be a mixed social.

A typical session lasts three days. The first day is travel followed by an afternoon session. If that's not logistically practical, an evening session. The next day is a full-day session; the third day concludes with a half-day session. This allows time to travel back home. When a resort facility is the venue and spouses attend, the meeting is extended to allow some additional social time.

If you are invited into an existing group, approach it with a positive and an open mind. If you can make the commitment, by all means join. If you're not currently in a group and you feel it would be good for you, try to locate others with similar feelings and start your own group.

If you are not in a study group, try it, you may like it.

L.8: ANNUAL CALENDAR

I am very disciplined by my personal calendar. I use every moment and I never lose control of the varied compartments in my life. I am very effective with the use of my time.

In October I purchase a large year-at-a-glance calendar. By the end of November I've completed a comprehensive schedule for the entire coming year.

In order to do this effectively, I make sure I have my priorities organized well in advance.

- I have a list of every industry and nonindustry meeting and convention I plan on attending.
- I have a list of all family events and occasions like birthdays, anniversaries, etc.
- I have a list of all my key business contacts: my best clients, my business associates and hot prospects I want to approach.
- I have a list of the personal and business goals that I hope to attain during the coming year with some idea of how much work time will be necessary to achieve those goals.
- I have an idea of how much time I want for rest and relaxation.
- I have a list of business trips scheduled for the coming year for meetings or speaking engagements. Since most are scheduled a year in advance, I rarely take on additional trips during the current calendar year.

With all that information available, it takes several days to manipulate the scheduling so everything is entered in the calendar. I also include open times for unplanned business opportunities. These open times will eventually be used for unexpected but necessary business needs, such as study groups, training sessions, schools or whatever seems appropriate.

Anticipated visits with clients and business associates are assigned at a specific time—such as breakfast, lunch or dinner—which is planned as much as 12 months in advance. This scheduling works because once my initial calendar is completed, and it's reasonably complete by November, I distribute it to the key people in my organization who might have scheduling conflicts that I'm not aware of. They get a chance to add to my calendar or change dates which sometimes requires some more juggling.

Finally my assistant, who has a duplicate diary and controls a good part of my life, makes all the adjustments and corrections. When I am convinced my schedule is reasonably complete, and by then it is a schedule for the entire organization, it is done on the computer with graphics showing key birthdays, holidays, conventions, meetings and special events. Each month is on a separate page with the twelve months constituting the full calendar year.

The calendar is distributed to key people in my organization by December. Each person who appears on the calendar, for one or more scheduled appointments, receives a personal letter listing the dates and times I expect to visit them during the following year. They may also receive an edited calendar, without my individual appointments included, but they know where I will be at any given time. That distributed calendar includes company and industry meetings they may want to attend.

I have been asked how I know a year in advance that I'll be able to keep a breakfast or a luncheon appointment. It's amazing how many I can keep exactly as scheduled. But to be safe, I don't fill in every day of every week. I deliberately leave at least one day a week completely clear to allow for flexibility. The schedule may not work precisely as originally distributed, but there is enough flex time built in so that a meeting can be rescheduled.

The advantage is that if I want to see someone and it's on the calendar, they know I care about them and I will see them. If it can't be at the predesignated time, it can be moved into flex time to suit either of our convenience, but it's never dropped.

Is this a system that others should implement? That's up to the individual. It works for me and if nothing else it may trigger an idea. If you don't want to do it for a full year perhaps a month at a time would be effective. At the very least you should be working three weeks in advance. This concept is a good skeleton on which to build your own system.

L.9: EAT EFFECTIVELY

You may think this section is about a proper diet, but it actually addresses the effective use of time. A long time ago I discovered that my breakfasts, lunches and dinners were left to happenstance. I would do my weekly planning the Thursday before the start of each week and block out specific times for prospecting, contacting, fact finding and closing. I rarely scheduled business-related meals. I eventually became aware that most people usually eat alone or with other "convenient" associates, so I changed my own scheduling.

At my weekly planning sessions, I identify people I want to meet with. Then I set up four breakfasts, four lunches and two dinners each week (supplementing those already scheduled in my annual calendar) with people directly related to my personal and business goals. I make certain they are not the same people over and over again. They might be clients, business associates, centers of influence, prospects, friends, family or whomever.

The reason I only schedule four breakfasts and four lunches is because it's not unusual for me to come across somebody that I want to have breakfast or lunch with in the course of the week. If I must reschedule an appointment, I have some flex time to accommodate changes. If I were completely booked, there would be no opportunity to make additional appointments. As a result of this program, during most working weeks I have five formal breakfasts and lunches and two dinners. I conclude most weeks with as many as 12 valuable interviews conducted under very pleasant circumstances, plus my other non-meal type interviews, that I would not have otherwise had.

This is an extremely simple but effective use of otherwise wasted time. I know salespeople who don't see 12 people a week under any circumstance, but I have 12 before I even begin the normal work time. Most of these eating opportunities reinforce an existing interrelationship or result in valuable achievements.

You can't help but grow as a person and in your business if you have 700 meetings a year, breaking bread with people who can have a favorable impact on your livelihood.

If you haven't already done so, consider eating more effectively.

L.10: CHANGE—THE PRICE OF SUCCESS

People who buy books like this hope to get usable ideas. In effect, they are not satisfied with the way things are.

Despite their good intentions they tend to stay in their same old ruts. But now and then their active minds will be triggered by something that lifts them from their rut.

Habits are hard to break and our present activities are as comfortable as an old pair of slippers. The new idea is usually outside of our comfort zone. The price of success is our accepting these ideas and implementing change.

I learned long ago that if I didn't use a new idea quickly, it was soon forgotten. Therefore, I force myself to try new ideas immediately. Over my lifetime I have tried thousands of things, most of which didn't work, so I didn't keep doing them. On the other hand, those that did work have become part of me.

I also learned that I had to give new ideas a fair chance to succeed. They say if you do something for 37 consecutive days, on the 38th day it is easier to do it than not do it. If it appeared to be a good idea I forced myself to do it for the magical 37 days, by which time it became me.

Finally, I learned that from every book and from every meeting I accumulated long lists of ideas. The result of this overload is I ended up doing nothing. Then I developed a star system. For example, after a meeting I would review my notes more objectively. Most notes reflected okay ideas but they were not significant enough to make them a priority. I filed those away for an appropriate occasion.

The few good ideas that stood out as having potential I starred in the left-hand margin. Really top-notch concepts got two stars. Those were started immediately.

Change is the price of success.

L.11: OVERVIEW OF TIME CONTROL

The secret of time management is to prioritize. Here are some key questions to determine if you should spend time on a specific activity:

- If this project is not done, will it reduce my career effectiveness?
- Can someone else do this for me, even if I could do it a little better myself?
- If I only get paid for certain accomplishments, can I afford to spend much of my limited available time on this particular activity?

For most salespeople the top priority is people contact. Until this is done on a daily basis, everything else is expendable.

In L.6 you read how important delegation is for time control. However, many people don't really delegate. Some keys to effective delegation include:

- Take the time to train the assistant properly.
- Monitor the work on a regular, scheduled basis.
- Let the assistant do the job, even if mistakes are made.
- Use all the time you save from delegation to work at your priority activity which is selling.
- Finally, don't bother delegating if you can't follow the points above!

On work days from 8 A.M. to 6 P.M., any time you spend other than in productive activity is a waste of valuable time. Attempt to spend every possible moment in front of an important person or on the phone talking to one. That means the paper-work and administration that you can't delegate away must be done at night or on weekends.

Remember, when an assistant can do a task correctly without your presence, you have maximized the value of delegation.

Have your assistant open all mail and categorize it in separate folders for efficiency. The folders include such categories as personal letters, business letters, company mail, industry mail, junk mail, bills and checks, client service, even accumulated phone messages.

More tips for time management:

- Train yourself not to touch the same piece of paper twice.
- Go through each folder, take the top piece of paper and finish it before touching the next.
- Don't browse through to find the good stuff.
- Finish each item in order, even if it means getting a file, getting a form and completing it immediately.
- Scan memos and toss most of them.
- Carry a TO DO list. Everything that must be done tomorrow, like the phone calls you couldn't complete, are transferred to the next day's list.
- Drop magazines and periodicals into your attaché case to be read at a future time.
- If the next issue of a magazine comes before you have read the last one, throw the old one away unread.
- Have a phone in your car so the next morning you can start contacting the people you couldn't reach the night before.
- If you are on the West coast, you can make Eastern calls as early as 6:00 A.M. On the East coast, Western calls can be made late into the evening.

- Schedule breakfast and lunch meetings almost every day and book them well in advance. You can have 8 of the 10 weekly opportunities committed before making your usual appointments.

L.12: MOBILE PHONES

At one time mobile phones were a novelty; today they are a necessity. Almost everyone in business has one. Either installed in the car or carried by the person, they are useful for incoming calls when you are away from the office. They are even more valuable for outgoing calls.

Making phone calls from the office is a necessary but inefficient use of time. Chances are you have wasted time going to or from the office, traveling between appointments or waiting for your next meeting. You can watch the scenery or listen to tapes, but why not use the time for calls?

Time spent commuting back and forth in the morning and evening can be converted to valuable time by making calls. This frees you to pursue priorities when you would otherwise be on the phone.

Incidentally, using that time for listening to tapes for education and motivation is also time well spent. But before you turn on the tape deck, catch up on the necessary phone calls. A to-do slip, updated daily, should list every phone call you have to make. Also carry both the home and office phone numbers of the significant people in your life. Program your mobile phone with numbers for those people you call regularly. When you get phone messages at the office, only call back during periods allocated for phone calls, or transfer that name and number to the to-do slip and call later from the car.

Of course, if the call sounds important, return it immediately.

Mobile phones can be a tremendous time saver. With intelligent planning, you can convert otherwise dead time into productive time.

L.13: TIME'S A-WASTING

Two hours wasted each work day add up to over 500 hours wasted per year. That adds up to 10 work weeks!

By working smarter and a little harder, you have more time to play and you accomplish more. It is amazing how little time is actually spent on productive, creative activities. A good exercise is to keep exact time records for one week, listing everything you do and how long it took. At the end of each day, count up the hours actually spent doing the really top priority activities in your life.

Unless you are unique in your self-discipline, you will probably find that you work less than one-third of the time you are away from home. Relatively minor adjustments in your schedule and work patterns might double your results with a minimum impact on your lifestyle.

Personalities who strive for independence or who have intense ambition often instinctively resist discipline, record keeping and organized work procedures.

Conversely, people who are instinctively disciplined, cautious and sensitive are often less motivated and successful. Although changing either personality is difficult, I would rather work with the aggressive, undisciplined type and teach them procedures. This is because disciplines are easier to change than motivation. However, both personalities can do it.

If you are a free spirit who hates procedures, force yourself to use systems in order to achieve maximum effectiveness.

If you are a systems person who lacks drive, force yourself out of your comfort zone and dream about living like a high achiever.

L.14: DON'T TOUCH IT TWICE

Sure signs that you're drowning in paper are:

- Mail is opened, read and put aside for future action.
- Correspondence, circulars and memorandums are accumulated for future reading.
- Paperwork is begun, put aside, restarted, again and again.
- Unpleasant tasks are accumulated for future action.
- It gets more difficult to quickly find something that is needed, which causes wasted time.
- Work accumulates cutting into efficiency and contributing to procrastination.
- Papers that have been read and touched over and over again become untimely and are thrown away.

Never touch the same piece of paper twice.
Early in my career I opened all the mail, read it and stacked some of it up for future action. The difficult things I deferred for later action. The simple things I went back to immediately. I handled each paper at least twice.

The more complicated tasks were reviewed day after day, and action was deferred for an indefinite time. A task that might normally take 10 minutes would compound itself into hours of postponements.

To attend to these tasks *immediately* is the most efficient use of time.

Now, when a piece of paper appears on my desk I will not even pick it up unless I plan to do something about it immediately. I initiate *and* complete the action that it demands. If I consider it unimportant, it goes directly into the waste basket or I delegate it to someone on my staff. This is a key part of efficiency.

In delegating items I either scribble right on the same piece of paper or use a "buck slip," a piece of paper attached with directions and information for routing. If more instructions are needed, I dictate onto a tape that is put in a folder with the entire pile of papers and given to my secretary who handles the matters from that point on. A tape may have one item or dozens of items on it, but when the stack leaves my desk, so do those papers. I don't touch them twice.

The items I can't throw away or delegate get my immediate attention. If they require phone calls, dictation or personal action, I take care of it before I pick up the next piece of paper. This may sound simple, but it requires a great deal of self-discipline. Procrastination is a powerful instinct and the curiosity about the next piece of paper is a tremendous draw. Yet, once this system is learned, the time that can be saved and the speed with which work can be completed is absolutely astonishing.

L.15: STRESS, PAPER AND TIME

There is always too much to do and not enough time to do it. In the old days I raced against the clock with a knot in my stomach. I could never catch up. I have not felt that knot for many years. Here's why.

1. I learned that if I can't finish something today, it will be there tomorrow.
2. I learned no one is indispensable and no one is forever.
3. I learned to prioritize my life and cut back on what I could do in a single day.
4. I learned to schedule my family, community and recreational time into every work week and made those times sacred.
5. I learned to let go by delegating duties.
6. I learned to set short- and long-term goals and systems to get the jobs done.

One system that probably has helped me more than any other in response to the blizzard of paper work is don't touch the same piece of paper twice, which was explained previously.

It is more difficult to learn and implement than it sounds. However, it can be mastered. It applies to everything: phone messages, mail, circular letters, magazines, bills, checks, letters and so on.

I taught my assistant to open all incoming mail and place it in manila folders by category. These folders are stacked on my desk. The folder for current messages gets priority attention. All other folders accumulate until specific allocated paper time is available. This is open-ended time, so there is no pressure to finish by a particular hour. I prefer to attack the paper piles two evenings a week. I don't open the first folder until I have private uninterrupted time. My wife knows not to expect me for dinner those nights.

I then take the papers and dispose of them immediately.

They can be thrown away, buck-slipped to someone else, responded to by dictation—whatever.

Before I leave the office every piece of paper is off my desk and I head home feeling good. It's efficient and eliminates stress. Despite my very busy and active schedule, I get all the paperwork done while my less organized peers are drowning in paper day and night. Systems do work.

Striving for success is a stressful business. Today's work load tests our long-term capacity to pace ourselves so we don't burn out. While longevity cannot be guaranteed, time spent on physical and mental well-being improves the odds for survival. Likewise, any stress-relieving system makes us more efficient and more productive which helps reduce stress.

L.16: TOO BUSY?

Watching salespeople all over the world has convinced me that those with the most clutter on their desks, the most paperwork yet undone, and the most work to take home every night, are usually not superstars. When you speak to them, they usually say they are swamped. They have barely enough time for sales interviews because they're so bogged down in minutiae.

If you ask any of these people to do something above and beyond their basic call of duty they invariably answer, "I wish I could, but I simply don't have the time."

Conversely, the most successful people seem to be totally organized, frequently have assistants, delegate most of the minutiae, concentrate on sales priorities and when you ask them to do something above and beyond the call of duty, almost without exception, they say, "Yes."

They are busier than the first group, but they're never too busy to do something else if it's important. They concentrate on priorities and relationships, not on paper and administration.

If you're working too hard and making too little, if you never have time to do what you want, if you haven't developed close interpersonal relationships in and out of the business, then it's time to re-evaluate where you're spending your time. Successful people always have time and conversely the unsuccessful people never seem to. That is not logical but it communicates a message. It's difficult to see ourselves objectively, but if the questions in the following Action Project describe your current situation, it is time to pay serious attention to time control and shift your time-related priorities.

ACTION PROJECT

Time Control

We all start each day with the same available time.

World-class salespeople have developed skills and disciplines that assure a maximum effectiveness from their working hours.

The following checklist identifies many time savers. It should be reviewed periodically. Although you may institute some of these ideas immediately, with the passage of time others may become appropriate.

Establish Priorities	Doing This	Implement	Postpone
1. 8:00 A.M. to 6:00 P.M. for people contacts, not paperwork.	_____	_____	_____
2. Use breakfast, lunch, dinner for one-on-one visits.	_____	_____	_____
3. Have weekly planning session to review past week and set up next week.	_____	_____	_____
4. Schedule adequate telephone time each week.	_____	_____	_____
5. Schedule paperwork sessions in evening or on weekends.	_____	_____	_____
6. Know how many interviews you require each week to achieve goals.	_____	_____	_____
7. Schedule planned family and/or recreation and physical well-being time.	_____	_____	_____
8. Schedule study and class time for educational growth.	_____	_____	_____

Establish Priorities   **Doing This   Implement   Postpone**

9. Carry goals on a 3 x 5 card as
   daily reminder of your "dreams."   _____   _____   _____

10. Do first priority things first each
    day.   _____   _____   _____

11. Practice—raise your skill level up
    to achieve more in less time. If you
    are a salesperson, try to reduce the
    length and number of interviews
    necessary to make a sale.   _____   _____   _____

Time Savers   **Doing This   Implement   Postpone**

1. Hire and train an assistant,
   and then delegate.   _____   _____   _____

2. Delegate anything that is not on
   your top priority list or that your
   assistant can do as well as or
   better than you.   _____   _____   _____

3. Have regular sessions with your
   assistant to follow up projects,
   train and monitor results.   _____   _____   _____

4. Learn to never touch the same
   piece of paper twice.   _____   _____   _____

5. Keep paper sessions open-ended
   so you can work until you have a
   clean desk.   _____   _____   _____

6. Have home phone numbers of all
   key contacts and associates available
   for nighttime administration and
   phone sessions.   _____   _____   _____

	Doing This	Implement	Postpone
7. Buy equipment that can make you more efficient:			
Mobile phone	_____	_____	_____
Pager	_____	_____	_____
Computer and get online	_____	_____	_____
Dictating equipment	_____	_____	_____
Fax machine, etc.	_____	_____	_____
8. Use boilerplate presentations and standard sales talks.	_____	_____	_____
9. Use company brochures and procedures and utilize them whenever possible.	_____	_____	_____
10. Give or delegate away prospects and clients who don't now justify your personal time and attention.	_____	_____	_____
11. Keep accurate records of all activity: prospecting, contacting, sales, etc., so you can critique past results and use them to more accurately make future changes and to predict future results.	_____	_____	_____
12. Set up systems for regular client contacts that don't involve much of your time:			
Birthday cards	_____	_____	_____
Regular newsletter	_____	_____	_____
Annual client reviews	_____	_____	_____
Gifts and/or Christmas cards	_____	_____	_____

	Doing This	Implement	Postpone
13. Make as many phone calls from your car as possible to save time.	_____	_____	_____
14. When you complete a sale try to sell something else or increase the sale immediately or on product delivery.	_____	_____	_____
15. Use a "things to do today" sheet as a checklist for every day and prepare a new one every night.	_____	_____	_____
16. Keep client and prospect records on computer or on a set manual card system.	_____	_____	_____

Financial Record Systems

	Doing This	Implement	Postpone
1. Put all financial records—check writing, tax records, budget, etc.— on computer. Software exists to make this time efficient.	_____	_____	_____
2. Use two sets of credit cards; one for business expenses, one for personal use.	_____	_____	_____
3. Keep two checking accounts; one for personal use, one for business.	_____	_____	_____
4. Have duplicate time schedule diaries; one for you, one for your assistant so you can be contacted at any time and so charges incurred can be cross-indexed to identify a business expense.	_____	_____	_____

Doing This   Implement   Postpone

5. Don't use cash unless absolutely
   necessary and then always get
   receipts.   _____   _____   _____

   Positive mental attitude, enthusiasm and time efficiency can make super successes.

   Smile as you work and remember: Two additional hours each work day equal 500 hours a year—that's an additional 10 weeks of productive effort. Use time control skills so when you work you produce. Then you'll be doing what world-class salespeople do. It's worth the effort.

Final Word:
Does Everybody Live?

Relationships and self-esteem bring happiness and success. A life of self-fulfillment and self-actualization is the ultimate human reward. Leaving your footsteps in the sands of time, while achieving your personal dreams and aspirations, is what keeps us going.

Interpersonal relationships, which are the foundation of relationship selling, are also the keystones that make the dream a reality.

To illustrate let me share a beautiful story about a very special couple who had a great impact on many lives, including mine. I'll call them Fred and Carol.

Fred was one of the greatest salesmen I've ever known. He was a church, community, college, industry and philanthropic volunteer leader. He was an author, speaker, tape and film producer who shared his skills and expertise without pay.

He was a devoted husband and father and raised children who became attorneys, judges and a bank president.

Carol was equally active and involved. She was always available for family obligations. They were inseparable and shared a great life.

During much of their mature life she battled cancer. At times it was disabling, at other times it was in remission. Fred was always there to support her when she needed him, and when she was up to it, she was there to support him. Their strength was in their pride and their relationships.

Everyone loved and admired them both. His clients enjoyed the most caring, sharing, love relationships with the two of them and reciprocated in kind. The protégés of both Carol and Fred were counted in the hundreds, including my wife Sandy and myself. They were never too busy for any worthwhile cause or for anyone in their world. Their family was number one, but there were lots of number twos not far behind.

The great sales success Fred enjoyed was a direct result of his high-touch, caring, sharing and loving relationships—plus his extraordinary expertise.

Life was good for them and they were happy as a result of high self-esteem and good interpersonal relationships.

When it came time to retire from business, Fred had become president of the company he represented. Retirement was an overstatement. Fred remained on the Board of Trustees of Notre Dame University, continued his philanthropic activities, was a leader in the national political party of his choice, continued to monitor other salespeople, spoke at meetings and continued to write.

The children were grown but remained the most important part of their lives.

One day my phone rang and Carol and Fred were both on the line. They called to tell Sandy and me that Fred had the early stages of Alzheimer's. They wanted to tell us personally, before it became obvious or we heard it from somebody else.

We were shocked and depressed. They assured us everything was as good as it could be, and they would fight it together. They promised to keep in touch.

I visited them when I could but it hurt to watch this super human being slowly fail. When Fred could no longer communicate, Carol called and said they were going to sell the New Jersey house and move close to Notre Dame. Carol told us the medical facilities were better there, family was closer, they both loved the area and it was the right thing to do.

She promised to be in touch when they arrived in South Bend and give us their new address and phone number.

Time passed and we heard nothing. Finally, one day their daughter called to let us know Carol had passed away. She then shared the whole story.

Carol, who attended Fred's every need, learned that her cancer had acted up again. Her time was limited. She only told her daughter and pledged her to secrecy. She was concerned with Fred's well-being after she was gone so she sold the house, went to South Bend and bought a new one, furnished it, hired full-time, round-the-clock nurses, then returned to New Jersey to pack and move Fred and their personal items.

In her dying days she moved Fred into the new house, got the nurses organized, then quietly and privately passed away.

I visited Fred in South Bend after learning of this extraordinary example of love. Fred recognized me and called me by my name, he talked about Carol like she was still with him. I took him to dinner on the Notre Dame campus and after dinner he said I should take him home because Carol was waiting and he didn't want to leave her alone. Love is stronger than Alzheimer's. They were still together.

Soon thereafter Fred passed on as well.

I loved them both. This was as beautiful a love story as Sandy and I have ever witnessed.

The point of sharing this is that it describes two people who made a tremendous positive difference to thousands of people, as well as the world in which we all live. It shows how a kind, gentle, caring person can be a whole human being while concurrently using those same attributes to be a super-successful business person.

Some people think business or selling are mutually exclusive with giving and kindness. Quite the contrary, they are interdependent. Great salespeople are great human beings.

Relationships and self-esteem make for happiness; Fred and Carol were very happy. They are gone but their contributions during their lifetimes live on in others. We all know that someday we all will die.

Although everyone accepts that irrefutable fact positive people don't dwell on death but happily smell today's flowers and learn to live for the moment.

A recent experience made me aware of a different perspective of life and death that is worth sharing.

Not long ago I had an amazing experience concerning two very special people in my sales organization. Both were young—one in his 40s, the other in his late 20s. Both had become very prosperous in a remarkably short time. They were my business associates and became my very good friends. In a weird coincidence, within a two-week period each of them asked to meet with me privately about what turned out to be very serious concerns.

The one in his 40s told me that he had just been diagnosed as HIV-positive. He was extremely frightened and terribly distraught. We talked for quite a while and eventually concluded the interview with a hug and my offer to be there if he needed me.

The younger man shared with me that he had just learned he had cancer of the liver and was going to need surgery and very possibly chemotherapy. Again, after a long emotional visit we concluded with a hug and my promise of support.

Subsequent to the visits, I observed two completely different reactions as they both faced life-threatening situations. The older individual who was HIV-positive became depressed and totally withdrew from our world. He stopped coming to the office and, when we did see him, he was disheveled, depressed and no longer shaved. He had developed a negative attitude, filed for total disability and disappeared from our lives.

We speak occasionally on the phone. He's in another world, with no mission, no direction and, apparently, no happiness. I love him and wish it was otherwise, but obviously it is beyond my control.

The younger man went through chemotherapy, several surgical procedures and every conceivable test and treatment available. At no time did he change his positive mental attitude and continued to live the same life he lived prior to the diagnosis. He was active in his college alumni group and remained a very positive social person within our organization. He continued to see clients and continued to sell products, and at least on the outside, seemed completely happy. He was trying to enjoy every moment. While he recognized the seriousness of his condition, he believed he could lick it. Even if he couldn't, it wasn't going to interfere with living life to the fullest. He never gave up on his dreams and aspirations.

All this began four years ago and I watched their stories evolve. The one who is HIV-positive is still alive and still out of our life but, happily, doing reasonably well. He probably hasn't lived a completely fulfilling day since the diagnosis. We never see him and I truly miss him, but he has chosen to disappear. He's a wonderful human being and a good friend, but he needs his own space and I'm not going to intrude.

Sadly, the younger one with cancer fought a great battle while living every day to the fullest, and despite his courage and positive mental attitude, succumbed a few months ago. He had been given two years by the doctors but lived a relatively happy and full life for almost four.

This whole experience has given me a new sense and realization about life. Everyone dies. But some people don't live. We don't know when our time will be up. I lost a two-year-old child, but I currently enjoy visiting with my mother-in-law who is 92.

Since we don't know and can't be sure when that final day of reckoning will come, it makes sense to use every moment we have to the fullest. I have seen young men in their 90s and old men in their 30s. I have observed people who have retired from life move into God's waiting room. They simply exist until they die.

The greatest single gift any of us will every receive is the right to life. What we do with that opportunity is a direct reflection of our own attitude.

The story of my two young, wonderful friends has had a tremendous impact on my own sense of value. We can't predict the future nor can we change the past, but we certainly can live one day at a time and try to enjoy every moment. The lessons to be learned from the stories in this concluding section accentuate everything in this book. Interpersonal relationships—family, social, professional—are the most important happenings in each of our lives. To cultivate and develop strong relationships and to make this world a better place is a mission we should all enthusiastically embrace.

The realization that we can make a difference in the lives of others contributes to our ability to determine our lifestyle. It gives us the strength to achieve our dreams. That is the magic of being the best you can be.

In closing, I hope each reader will take the information in this book and use it to fit his own individual situation. Whether you're a professional salesperson or in an entirely different persuasion, the principles, methods and skills contained herein are adaptable and transferable to any individual in any situation.

Success and happiness are a direct result of self-esteem and relationships. The great majority of people profess to wanting success, happiness, self-esteem and good interpersonal relationships. Relatively few people are precluded from such a dream by physical or mental restrictions. However, far too many people who can truly be all they want to be, will never fully achieve success and happiness because they simply will not pay the price.

That price is change. In other words, selling themselves on themselves. *Do* instead of trying. Treat others with silk gloves, not brass knuckles. That's what successful people do.

I wish you great happiness.

Biographical Capsule

Norman Levine, though educated in ecology, became a salesman when he couldn't find a job in his chosen profession. He initially sold many products—including Fuller brushes—but he is now president of the Levine Financial Group in San Francisco, California. He is a family man, and is active in numerous organizations in the fields of politics, wildlife ecology, sports and industry, as well as many philanthropies.

After 50 years in the selling business, Norman Levine is an expert in sales procedure and technique. His industry positions include past president of the National Association of Life Underwriters (NALU), past president of the General Agents and Managers Association (GAMA), past chairman of the Life Underwriters Training Council (LUTC), member of the American Society of Chartered Life Underwriters and member of the Million Dollar Round Table (MDRT).

Norman Levine is a world-renowned public speaker who has spoken in all 50 states and 23 international countries. He is the recipient of numerous insurance awards and is listed in *Who's Who in America* and *Who's Who in Insurance*. He was inducted into the GAMA Hall of Fame and has the highest individual honor that the life insurance industry bestows, the John Newton Russell Award.

Other books by Norman Levine include *Yes, You Can, How to Build a $100,000,000 Agency in Five Years or Less* and *From Life Insurance to Diversification,* all of which have been translated into several languages and are sold worldwide. Twenty of Norman Levine's audiotapes and videotapes are distributed worldwide on the subjects of salesmanship, management and being the best you can be.

Using This Guide

Blind spots or an existing prejudice may be the reason a person has been unable to identify or solve an existing problem. Therefore, it is absolutely necessary that the reader utilize this book with a disciplined, open mind. A closed mind is the major problem that keeps most people from correctly identifying the problem and finding a solution.

For example, I often hear sales professionals say they have poor closing skills. They concentrate on improving their power closing techniques in a futile effort to improve sales effectiveness. When I visit with such people we often find that the real problem was not closing techniques but something completely different. Once the problem is identified and addressed, the salesperson makes great progress in productivity and success.

Poor closing techniques can really be because of apparently unrelated issues such as poor prospects, weak interpersonal relationships, poor techniques to uncover the prospect's wants and needs, or inappropriate solutions to address the prospect's problems.

To get the most from this guide, the reader must take the time to honestly investigate areas previously taken for granted. These may give important insights to the real problem and solution. There may, in fact, be several unidentified issues that in combination will explain the real problem and provide several possible solutions.

The following cross-indexed guide lists several different concepts that may be relevant to the reader's apparent concerns. All those sections should be carefully read, even if they appear irrelevant. The reader must then do serious and objective introspection to see if there may be a clue as to the real problem and/or solution.

Learning the skills necessary to be a super salesperson will be a great advantage to anyone who wants to succeed in all people-related activities. You cannot lose a sale or earn a relationship because you are overqualified. You can lose in some interpersonal relationships because you took too much for granted or did not know how to handle a situation beyond your current level of expertise. The moral of that situation is to learn to be a sensitive and effective communicator, negotiator and salesperson, capable of handling anything, at any time, with smooth and cool *savoir-faire,* regardless of the position you currently hold, or to which you aspire.

The one certainty in life is, no matter how things are today, you will be exposed to lots of changes in the future. Be prepared.

Here are some typical concerns of people who want to succeed but are not totally satisfied with their present results. The letters and numbers following each situation refer to the section, concepts or action projects that should be carefully read. The concerns are separated into two categories. The first will be of interest to all readers, and the other probably of greater concern to professional salespeople. Refer to the contents for the page number.

OF GENERAL INTEREST

_____ I don't have enough friends.
A-7,8; A-AP; B-3,8,9; B-AP; D-1,3; D-AP; F-10,17; F-AP;
G-4; G-AP; I-3,5,11

_____ I have trouble interrelating with new contacts at social
functions.
A-3,7,8; B-3,9,12,14; B-AP; D-6; D-AP; F-7,10,17; G-4;
G-AP; H-3,6; I-3,5,11; L-9,10

_____ I don't seem to have real goals that motivate me.
A-2,7; A-AP; B-1,4,5,8,14; C-3; D-1,2,3,4,5,6; D-AP;
E-4,6,7; L-10

_____ Some days I just don't feel like going to work and I
think about quitting.
A-entire section; B-3,4,5,6,15; C-1,3,4,5; D-1,2,3,6;
D-AP; E-4,6,7; L-1,2,10,11

_____ I can't get people to follow my lead.
A-1,2,3,5,7,10,11; A-AP; B-2,8,9,12,15; B-AP; C-AP

_____ I get bogged down in details and can't do things I
really like.
C-2,3,4; D-1,2,3,4,6; D-AP; E-1,2,4,6,7; L-1,2,4,6,10,11;
L-AP

_____ I don't want to be so aggressive that I offend people.
A-1,7,8; B-3,9,14,15; G-AP; H-3,6; I-3; J-7; J-AP

_____ I don't keep records—I don't think I need them.
D-5; E-AP; L-4,5,10; L-AP

_____ I can't get people to open up to me.
A-2,3,5,7,8,10,11; A-AP; B-9,12,14,15; B-AP; F-9,10;
H-2,3,6; I-2,3,5,6,12

_____ I don't think I need more education.
A-5; B-12,15; E-4,6; H-1

_____ I am uncomfortable with successful or powerful people.
A-entire section; B-2,8,9,12,15; F-9,10; I-3,5,6,11

_____ How can I be successful in business and still have time for family, community, charities, recreation, etc.?
C-1,5,7; L-1,2,6,9,10,11,16; L-AP

_____ I am burned out and bored.
A-2,3,7,14; A-AP; B-3,4,6,7,14; B-AP; C-entire section; L-AP

_____ My spouse is unsupportive.
A-2,3,7,8,12; A-AP; B-3,6,15; C-5,6,7; D-1,3; D-AP

_____ I can't afford an assistant.
A-12; B-4; C-2; C-AP; D-3; L-1,6,10,11; L-AP

_____ It is easier for me to do it myself than to hire and train an assistant.
A-14; B-7,9,14; C-2,4,7; E-4,5,6; K-AP; L-1,2,6,11,13,14; L-AP

_____ I am often tired or depressed.
A-2,3,7,14; B-1,3,9; C-entire section

ESPECIALLY FOR SALES PROFESSIONALS

_____ I don't have enough people to see.
A-3,4; A-AP; B-4,9,14; B-AP; D-3,4; D-AP; E-entire section; F-entire section; G-entire section

_____ I get names of prospects but they won't see me.
A-2,3,7,8; A-AP; D-3,4; F-1,2,4,5,6,7,9,10,12,13,14; G-entire section; H-3,4,6,7; K-1,2,4,5; K-AP

_____ I often get stood up for scheduled appointments.
A-2,3,4,7,8; A-AP; B-5,6,7,9,14; B-AP; F-2,3,4,5,6,9,12

_____ I can't seem to be able to close cases.
A-2,3,5,7,8,9,10,11; A-AP; B-1,2,3,5,9,12,15; F-4,6,12;
H-1,2,3,6,7,8,9; I-2 through 16; I-AP; J-entire section

_____ I often get postponed by procrastinators.
A-2,3; A-AP; F-4,6,9; H-6,8,9; I-7,8,12,13,14,15; I-AP;
J-entire section

_____ People keep telling me they can't afford it.
A-AP; F-4,6,8,9; H-3,6,7,9; I-3,7,12,13,14,15,16; I-AP;
J-2,3,4,5,7; J-AP

_____ I haven't enough time to sell because of all the
paperwork.
C-2; D-4; E-2,3,4,7; H-5; I-17; L-entire section

_____ My sales are consistently smaller than my associates'
and competitors'.
A-2; B-7,8,12,14, B-AP, D-entire section; E-4; F-4,6,8,9;
H-1,2,8; J-4

_____ I can't get referred leads.
A-2,3,4,5,7,8; A-AP; B-15; F-1,2,3,4,5,6,7,8,9,10,12,13,14;
F-AP; G-4; G-AP; K-entire section

_____ My products are not competitive.
A-1,2,3,7; B-6,9; D-AP; F-4,5,7,8,9; H-7,8,9;
I-7,8,12,13,14,15; J-entire section

_____ My interviews take too long and it takes me too many
interviews to make a sale.
E-1,2,4; H-1,2,3,4,7,10; I-1,3,17; I-AP; J-2,3,4,6,7; J-AP;
L-3,9,10,11,13; L-AP

_____ I can't seem to get existing customers to buy again.
B-14; F-6; H-3; K-entire section

_____ I am uncomfortable calling on friends or relatives.
A-2,3,8; A-AP; D-4; F-4,6,7,9,14,15; G-4; G-AP;
I-2,3,6,12

_____ My problem is my company or product is no good.
A-2,3,7,14; A-AP; B-2,5,6,9,11; D-6; E-4,7; J-4; L-7,10

_____ I can't comfortably approach and sell the upscale,
richer, bigger market place.
A-entire section; B-7,9,12,14,15; B-AP; D-2,3; D-AP;
E-2; F-8,9,10,17

_____ I don't feel qualified to address certain desirable markets.
A-4,5,7,9,10,14; B-11,12,14,15; B-AP; D-1,2,3; D-AP;
E-3; F-6,7,8,9,10,17; H-2,3,4,6,8,9; I-2,3

_____ Classes, studying, meetings are a waste of my time.
I want to be out selling.
A-5; B-11,14,15; D-6; D-AP; E-4; E-AP; H-1,2; I-6; J-6;
L-3,6,7,16